Evangelical Christian Executives

Lewis D. Solomon

Evangelical Christian Executives

A New Model for Business Corporations

Transaction Publishers
New Brunswick (U.S.A.) and London (U.K.)

Copyright © 2004 by Transaction Publishers, New Brunswick, New Jersey.

All rights reserved under International and Pan-American Copyright Conventions. No part of this book may be reproduced or transmitted in any form or by any means, electronic or mechanical, including photocopy, recording, or any information storage and retrieval system, without prior permission in writing from the publisher. All inquiries should be addressed to Transaction Publishers, Rutgers—The State University, 35 Berrue Circle, Piscataway, New Jersey 08854-8042.

This book is printed on acid-free paper that meets the American National Standard for Permanence of Paper for Printed Library Materials.

Library of Congress Catalog Number: 2004046098
ISBN: 0-7658-0230-9
Printed in Canada

Library of Congress Cataloging-in-Publication Data

Solomon, Lewis D.
    Evangelical Christian executives : a new model for business corporations / Lewis D. Solomon.
        p. cm.
    Includes bibliographical references and index.
    ISBN 0-7658-0230-9 (alk. paper)
        1. Executives. 2. Leadership—Religious aspects—Christianity. 3. Business ethics. 4. Stewardship, Christian. I. Title.

HD38.2.S65   2004
261.8'5—dc22   2004046098

For my wife Janet, with love

Contents

Acknowledgments

As is the case with most books, one person is listed as the author, but many made it happen. I want to express my thanks to a number of corporate leaders who read and commented on portions of the manuscript: John Beckett, Steven Bono, Edward Cochrane, Max DePree, Kathy Lazar, Suzanne Lee, Norm Miller, R.B. Pamplin, Jr., C. William Pollard, Henry Rogers, Mark Schurman, Craig Shoal, and Rich Towe. Nell B. Taylor and Ferial de Lumen diligently typed the manuscript through its many drafts. Without the tireless efforts of Matthew Mantel, Reference Librarian, The Jacob Burns Law Library, The George Washington University Law School, this work would not have come to fruition.

1

Introduction: The Crisis in Corporate Leadership and Governance

Business is the dominant social institution in the United States (and globally) at the beginning of the twenty-first century. Corporations, not nation states, control the world's economy. The vast majority of individuals in the United States work for private sector organizations.

A corporation's reputation is built, in part, on honesty—telling the truth in its communications and dealings with others—and integrity—doing what is right regardless of the consequences. For corporate executives, integrity connotes the courage to hold to one's convictions and remain true to oneself and to implement policies and practices in accordance with these convictions.

In the early years of the twenty-first century, many weeks were marked by a firm's or its top executive's reputation exploding, splattering the public, in general, and shareholders and investors, in particular, with frustration, disillusionment, and a deep loss of trust and confidence. Thousands of employees lost their jobs and pensions. Corporations confessed to cooking their books; the reputation of once-respected accounting firms has been tarnished. In short, now familiar litany, Enron, WorldCom, Adelphia, and Arthur Anderson, among other corporate scandals, names indelibly etched in the business hall of shame, created a public backlash against business and its captains.

The ethic of greed and deceit in the marketplace came under intense scrutiny, unmatched since the 1930s. Business executives, once granted near superstar status, became the stuff of ridicule and disdain.

In commenting on the demonizing of corporate managers in the summer of 2002, Andrew S. Grove, chairman of Intel Corp., wrote:

1

I grew up in Communist Hungary. Even though I graduated from high school with excellent grades, I had no chance of being admitted to college because I was labeled a "class alien." What earned me this classification was the mere fact that my father had been a businessman. It's hard to describe the feelings of an 18-year-old as he grasps the nature of a social stigma directed at him. But never did I think that, nearly 50 years later and in a different country, I would feel some of the same emotions and face a similar stigma.

Over the past few weeks, in reaction to a series of corporate scandals, the pendulum of public feeling has swung from celebrating business executives as the architects of economic growth to condemning them as a group of untrustworthy, venal individuals....

I am proud of what our company has achieved. I should also feel energized to deal with the challenges of today, since we are in one of the deepest technology recessions ever. Instead, I'm having a hard time keeping my mind on our business. I feel hunted, suspect—a "class alien" again.

I know I'm not alone in feeling this way. Other honest, hard-working and capable business leaders feel similarly demoralized by a political climate that has declared open season on corporate executives and has let the faults, however egregious, of a few taint the public perception at all. This is just at a time when their combined energy and concentration are what's needed to reinvigorate our economy. Moreover, I wonder if the reflexive reaction of focusing all energies on punishing executives will address the problems that have emerged over the past year.[1]

Alan Greenspan, chairman, Board of Governors, Federal Reserve System, in his semiannual report to the United States Senate Banking Committee, captured the ethos of material self-aggrandizement that prevailed in the late 1990s. He pointed to a corporate culture blighted by "infectious greed" that seemed to grip much of the business culture as the cause of the breakdown in investor confidence. One key factor, according to Greenspan, was the plethora of stock options given to top executives. Knowing that stock option grants made executives' wealth almost entirely dependent on their respective firm's stock price, top managers had an incentive to improve the profits they reported. By pushing and manipulating a firm's financial numbers, they drove up stock prices, allowing executives to cash in their options. In other words, stock options enabled managers to get rich if they inflated or even faked profits and a few did. Greenspan stated:

An infectious greed seemed to grip much of our business community....Too many corporate executives sought ways to "harvest" some of those stock market gains [from the rapid increase of stock prices in the late 1990s]. As a result, the highly desirable spread of shareholding and options among business managers perversely created incentives to artificially inflate reported earnings in order to keep stock prices high and rising....The incentives they created overcame the good judgment of too many corporate managers. It is not that humans have become any more greedy than in generations past. It is that the avenues to express greed had grown so enormously.[2]

In a climate of fear and distrust and with the corner suite becoming scandal central, even honest executives came to obsess about the worst possible outcome of every business decision. The "CEO class," as one prominent journalist put it, became "seized by risk aversion....CEOs are hunkering down at the threat of jail. As a class they're under legal, political and societal assault, brought about by apparent crimes of a few of their peers, a general impression of excess by imperial CEOs and, of course, the collapse in share values after the boom from mid-1999 to mid-2000."[3]

In place of the do-anything-to-succeed mentality of the 1990s characterized by a maniacal focus on maximizing short-term profits in any possible way and at all costs as well as a focus on day-to-day, never mind quarterly, stock price fluctuations, came a new search for corporate purpose and executive leadership. Beyond beating earnings projections as the only goal for publicly held firms, more businesses came to realize that to be sustainable and profitable in the long run, they must establish objectives and adopt (and implement) values beyond mere profitability. In striving to build something lasting, more and more corporate executives came to ask: What is the role of business in society? What is the relationship between a firm and its shareholders, employees, customers, suppliers, and the communities in which it operates? Can you run a business that respects human beings and achieves true and lasting relationships with its employees, customers, suppliers, and the broader community, without sacrificing profits?

The Enduring, but Fundamental, Questions

The debate over corporate goals and stakeholder interests reaches well back into the twentieth century. Defenders of a narrower set of corporate goals and constituency interests argue that corporations should be concerned exclusively with maximizing the profits they can earn for their shareholders within the law and measuring performance on the basis of increasing share prices. Critics maintain that for-profit business corporations should be more "responsible" and that they should take account of all constituencies affected by their operations.

In the early 1930s, two leading corporate law scholars, Adolf A. Berle and E. Merrick Dodd, debated the role of the corporation. Berle's view was that corporate powers were held in trust and were "at all times exercisable only for the ratable benefit of the shareholders."[4] Dodd's thesis was that the business corporation was properly seen "as an economic institution which has a social service as well as a profit-making function."[5] But as Berle later astutely observed, the effect of the discussion was to recognize that "modern directors are not limited to running business enterprise for maximum profit, but are in fact and recognized in law as administrators of a community system."[6]

However, Professor Dodd's "managerialism" view, because it treats corporate managers as professionals whose duties require the exercise of almost statesmanlike responsibility, came under attack, most notably by Nobel laureate Milton Friedman. Looking to maximizing shareholder value based on the premise that shareholders are the only stakeholders in a business organization, Friedman stated in his landmark book, *Capitalism and Freedom*:

> [T]here is one and only one social responsibility of business—to use its resources and engage in activities designed to increase its profits so long as it stays within the rules of the game, which is to say, engage in open and free competition without deception or fraud.[7]

It remains unclear whether Friedman merely wanted corporate managers to stay within the law, or whether his use of the phrase "rules of the game" refers to some broader obligations. Subsequently, in a celebrated newspaper article, Friedman suggested that the "responsibility" of business is "to make as much money as possible while conforming of the basic rules of society, both those embodied in law and those embodied in ethical custom."[8] Beyond these linguistic quagmires, Friedman has come to represent the view that the sole responsibility of corporations is to make increasing profits for their shareholders.

In looking beyond short-term profit maximization for the sole benefit of shareholders, executives with a broader mindset often find comfort in the American legal framework, where courts have given firms considerable flexibility in undertaking socially responsible activities. In one leading case, the New Jersey Supreme Court upheld as valid a corporate charitable contribution to Princeton University, on the grounds that the gift at least arguably advanced the donor corporation's long-run business interests.[9] Thus, while retaining the profit maximization and efficiency goals of free market economists, the more moderate and flexible corporate governance model considers the time frame for assessing profitability to encompass long-term corporate profit and shareholder gain, and also enlarges the scope of corporate conduct. Under this approach, the use of corporate funds for philanthropic, humanitarian, or educational purposes does not require the showing of a likely, direct benefit. Rather, courts have recognized the allocation of corporate resources for one of these purposes as an end in itself, regardless of corporate benefit, on the ground that this type of corporate activity maintains and sustains a healthy social system that necessarily serves a long-run corporate purpose.[10]

In 1977, the American Law Institute (ALI), a nonprofit group devoted to the improvement of the law through restatement and reform of legal principles, embarked on a project to unify the basic standards of corporate governance, especially in areas not addressed by state corporation statutes. Many areas of the project proved controversial. However, in 1993, after more than fifteen years, the project came to a conclusion when the ALI approved the final version of its *Principles of Corporate Governance* (*Principles*). In reflecting the need to consider the long-term, broad gauge corporate interests, the section of the *Principles* dealing with the objective and conduct of the corporation provides:

(a)...[A] corporation...should have as its objective the conduct of business activities with a view to enhancing corporate profit and shareholder gain.

(b) Even if corporate profit and shareholder gain are not thereby enhanced, the corporation, in the conduct of its business: (1) Is obliged, to the same extent as a natural person, to act within the boundaries set by law; (2) May take into account ethical considerations that are reasonably regarded as appropriate to the responsible conduct of business; and (3) May devote a reasonable amount of resources to public welfare, humanitarian, educational, and philanthropic purposes.[11]

In the context of this flexible legal framework, many corporate executives increasingly see that firms must deal fairly with their employees, customers, and others (such as suppliers) to remain viable and succeed financially. For these leaders, as corporate stewards entrusted with protecting the interests of various groups, the term "stakeholder" has come to encompass all the individuals, groups, and institutions that affect or are affected by a business organization. They must build and sustain authentic relationships with their firm's various stakeholders.

Striving to orient their approach to corporate governance around multiple stakeholders: shareholders, employees, suppliers, customers, the surrounding communities, and various levels of government, modern managers realize their businesses must produce high quality products or services and provide employees with a work environment conducive to their personal growth and development while at the same time increasing shareholder wealth. But how can a business entity go about resolving these often-conflicting goals? It's not an either-or proposition. Rather, the religious faith and values of evangelical Christian executives provide a way of thinking about managing modern business corporations.

Evangelical Christian Executives Bring Their Religious Faith and Values to Their Corporations

This book focuses on the reconceptualization on the goals and stakeholders of modern business corporations. This time of doubt provides an unparalleled opportunity for a fundamental reexamination of the for-profit business corporation. Specifically, I want to examine the two longstanding questions: in whose interest and to what ends should corporations be run? Some executives have sought to go beyond Friedman's arguments that the only responsibility of business is to make a lawful profit and increase shareholder wealth—with shareholders as a business organization's only stakeholders or the ALI's approach that permits managers to take into account ethical considerations as well as public welfare, humanitarian, and philanthropic purposes. These corporate leaders have sought, and others in the future may seek, to bring religious faith and values into the workplace and their corporations. As Charles (Chuck) Colson, a Watergate co-conspirator, reborn as an evangelical Christian, who serves as chairman of Prison Fellowship Ministries (an organization designed to lead prisoners to Jesus, help them grow in their religious faith, and equip them to be responsible and productive citizens on their release) stated:

I stand as living proof that cure comes not from laws and statutes but from the transforming of the human heart—the embracing of a moral code to which conscience is bound. The real hope for corporate America lies in cultivating conscience, a disposition to know and do what is right....

The alternative is to take a bracing dose of reality, to recognize that the enemy is moral relativism and confusion, to embrace once again a solid code by which morality can be informed and then to go about the business of strengthening the conscience of the nation.[12]

This book focuses on evangelical Christians who founded or led (or currently lead) American business corporations. Some were executives with a strong, but private, religious faith. Others sought to weave religion, specifically their brand of religion, into the fabric of a business, building their religious faith into a corporation's culture, values, and strategies. This second group sought their firms to function and achieve business success according to Christian values, as they perceived them. They sought to integrate the worlds of faith and business. While realizing that a business has an obligation to compete and achieve a profit, they looked to achieve a cluster of objectives, with making a profit as only one corporate purpose. Their religious faith led many to a profound distance from the goal of profit on which others place ultimate value. According to John D. Beckett, CEO and chairman of R. W. Beckett Corp. (profiled in detail in chapter 8), "I have never really equated success with just the bottom line of profit and loss. Profit is a by-product of a healthy business but my first priority is to honor God with my company and take care of my people along the way."[13]

Some evangelical executives view the Bible as a divine management policy manual, a wellspring of practical truth, guidance, and inspiration. They view their success in the corporate world as due to a belief in and their implementation of biblical principles in the conduct of their businesses.

Again, John D. Beckett serves as an example of the relevance of a biblical approach to business. At one time, he parked his faith-based ideas at the office door when he went to work. He did not see how they applied to the rough-and-tumble world of business. "But I have now discovered", he stated, "how valuable it is to integrate enduring, biblically rooted truths into my work. They have benefited our company tremendously."[14]

In this book, I want to examine, from a corporate governance perspective, how senior executives brought evangelical Christianity into their businesses, particularly those who sought to guide their firms through their religious faith and values. I strive to encapsulate the beliefs and business approaches of these evangelical executives, without endorsing or denigrating them. Personally, I believe that Jesus was a Hebrew prophet, neither the son of God nor the path to salvation in this life or the hereafter.[15]

I will assess, where possible, the impact of incorporating religious faith and values into the corporate principles and practices. Specifically, from a bottom line, results-oriented viewpoint, the book will assess how this approach impacts not only on profitability but also five other aspects: first, employee satisfaction (turnover and retention) and productivity as well as levels of executive compensation; second, product and service quality and customer satisfaction; third, legal compliance in general; fourth, environmental consciousness and environmentally-friendly practices within the context of a specific business; and fifth, the level of charitable giving.

There is a tension, hopefully, a creative tension, not necessarily a balance, between: first, a corporation's economic objective and the demands of the business world; and second, a commitment to Christian values, notably, love, and compassion, striving to understand and empathize with others and express kindness and think kind thoughts toward everyone. After Jesus indicated that the greatest commandment is loving God, He completed the directive stating, "The second is this: 'Love your neighbor as yourself.'" (Mark 12:31). The search for the fair treatment of non-shareholder stakeholders, including employees, customers, suppliers, and the surrounding communities, offers integrative possibilities for creatively reconciling, not balancing or compromising, seemingly opposing forces to steer a "true" course. According to business ethicist Laura L. Nash, the creative tension between the quest for profit and Christian teachings as well as the biblical demand to submit to God's will leads to the "creation of third alternatives that are more in line with biblical values and that often are strokes of economic brilliance as well."[16] I will explore how these firms went about (and whether they succeeded), as Nash put it, "creatively expanding the context in which...tradeoffs are encountered by reworking the process of value creation to take into account long-term fluctuations that a morally legitimate approach can be found"[17] and how this creative phenomenon and the reframing of business problems "leads to productive economic activity and to productive personal spiritual fulfillment."[18] In short, I want to examine how evangelical executives found a way to integrate competing, and seemingly divergent, aims, business and religious.

Overview of the Book

This book consists of four parts. First, in chapter 2 I briefly summarize the orientation of evangelical Christian business executives. Some have a private faith; they take a low-key approach in a corporate context. While offering a brief example of Jeffrey H. Coors, the head of Graphic Packaging International Corp., as illustrative of this group of executives, the chapter examines (and the book focuses on) the leadership styles of two other groups. One group, as preachers, weaves their religious faith into the fabric of their businesses. Building on their desire to bear witness to Jesus and to share the Gospel with others, they want to proselytize non-believers. A second group, using a more sophisticated approach, based on the biblical principles of stewardship or servant-leadership (or both concepts), actively pursues a values-management strategy.

I then present three models—constant, transformational, and evolving—of what it means for evangelical Christians to run a business. Despite being located at different points on the constant—transformational—evolving spectrum, all six of the firms I discuss in detail have emphasized something beyond mere profitability. Furthermore, all have achieved long-term success and viability.

Chapters 3 and 4 focus on two corporations, what I call constant firms, Covenant Transport, Inc. and R. B. Pamplin Corp., continually managed with a religious-orientation from their founding to the present day. At the outset, it is useful to note that throughout this book, I use the term "religion" to refer to institutional (and thus organized) rituals and dogma, with precept and beliefs derived from a text, the Bible, particularly focusing on salvation beyond this earthly existence.[19] Often a "precipitating crisis,"[20] some intense difficulty, led to a desire to confront this major event (or events), to successfully surmounting it (or them), followed by a personal transformation and a desire to implement an often newfound (or rediscovered) institutionalized system of religious faith and values in a business context and through concrete business policies and practices. As we will see, many of the executives profiled in this book encountered some type of precipitating crisis that profoundly changed not only their lives but also their approach to business.

David R. Parker, the founder, controlling shareholder, and chief executive officer and chairman of Covenant Transport, Inc., a publicly held entity analyzed in chapter 3, is a preacher-leader. The firm manifests Parker's evangelical style to its employees and customers.

In chapter 4, the privately-held R. B. Pamplin Corp. illustrates the stewardship leadership style of its head, R.B. Pamplin, Jr. Charitable giving, based on the biblical principle of tithing, serves as the keynote of this firm's enduring Christian orientation.

Then, in chapters 5 and 6, I turn to two corporations, which I
classify as transformational firms, The ServiceMaster Co. and Herman
Miller, Inc., that have undergone a transition over the years, moving
from a religious-based (or at least, in the case of Herman Miller, a
business led by evangelical Christians) to a more spiritual- or even a
secular-orientation. Although no agreed upon definition of "spiritual" exists, in this work I use the term to refer to a personal journey,
a quest if you will, encompassing: the search for meaning and purpose in life (including who am I, who are we, where are we going,
the contemplation of the problems of evil, pain, and suffering); an
awareness of timeless virtues (love, compassion, hope, and opti-
mism); a feeling of interconnectedness (and the sacredness) of everything and everyone, with everything and everyone, affecting (and
being affected by) everything else; a curiosity about the nature of
life and forces larger than oneself including a search for commun-
ion with and sense of awe in the presence of some sort of transcendent force, whether called, God, a Higher Power, or Spirit.[21] Spirituality is non dogmatic; it is not about proselytizing or converting
people to a particular belief system. Rather, it is universal, broadly
inclusive, and characterized by openness.

As developed in chapter 5, ServiceMaster, a successful publicly
held *Fortune* 500 corporation, grew from humble roots, led first by
a preacher-steward-leader and then by a succession of CEOs, who
combined preacher-steward-servant leadership styles. More recently,
this transitional firm, now led by a non-evangelical CEO, follows an
inclusive, non-sectarian approach. Coincidentally with this transition, the company's legal difficulties mounted and its financial results stagnated.

For decades, a family of evangelicals, who pursued a progressive
managerial approach, combining stewardship and servant-leadership, led Herman Miller a publicly owned *Fortune* 1000 corporation, considered in chapter 6, to preeminence in the office furniture
industry. As management passed out of this family's hands, a new,
secular CEO has pursued a modern financially and operationally
disciplined style, while continuing to emphasize environmental consciousness.

Next, in chapters 7 and 8, I consider two firms, what I call an
evolving companies, Interstate Batteries System of America, Inc. and
R. W. Beckett Corp., each of which started as a secular organization
but evolved into religious-based entities. A secular-orientation, for

purposes of this book, refers to a universal human values orientation, focusing on love, truthfulness, tolerance, responsibility, courage, and wisdom, or even an earth- or nature-centered approach.[22]

The privately held Interstate Batteries discussed in chapter 7,
evolved from a secular firm to one with a pronounced religious-
orientation. Under the leadership of a CEO, Norman (Norm) Miller,
who combined preacher and steward leadership styles, it achieved
success in the replacement battery market, along with employee satisfaction and a high level of charitable giving.

The privately owned Beckett Corp., examined in chapter 8, attained dominance in another mundane field, burners for residential
oil furnaces. With a change in top management under tragic circumstances, under a new CEO, John D. Beckett, the son of the founder,
who combined stewardship and servant-leadership styles, it evolved
from a secular-entity to a religiously based firm. It is known for its
enlightened management practices that have generated extraordinary
enthusiasm among its employees and loyalty to the organization.

Finally, in chapter 9, I offer a brief conclusion focusing on what
other American business corporations can learn from the six firms
and their executives analyzed in this work. Existing business entities, even giant publicly held firms, if blessed by the inspired leadership of their top executives, such as Ken Melrose, chairman and
CEO of The Toro Company a *Fortune* 1000 corporation, who provide vision, direction, and guidance, can infuse values into the organization and achieve beneficial results for multiple stakeholders.
An organization striving to find answers to the perplexing corporate
governance questions raised in this book must undertake a strategic
planning process, focusing on developing a mission statement and a
core values statement, with input from its directors, executives, and
employees. The difficulties of organization change should not, however, be minimized.

At the outset let me state my thesis. The six firms detailed in this
work demonstrate that executives can successfully lead businesses
with goals beyond short-term profit maximization for their shareholders. Business organizations can successfully meet multiple aims,
combining both financial profitability and other, broad goals, such
as serving the needs of non-shareholder constituencies, including
employees, customers, suppliers, and the community at-large. The
human side and the financial side of a business are not mutually
exclusive. CEOs need not have a tunnel-vision preoccupation with

bottom-line profits to satisfy the short-term expectations of the investment community. In addition to focusing on the human dimensions of business, based on each individual's dignity and worth and deeply valuing people, John D. Beckett noted, "We've also been able to produce above-average profits and excellent returns to the shareholders."[23]

In some instances, the returns generated by these faith-based corporations have been phenomenal. For example, from 1987 through 1995, ServiceMaster, a corporation in the low technology business of providing cleaning and other services to institutional and residential clients, "earned an average return on shareholders' equity of almost 82 percent, a much higher return than was earned by either Intel or Microsoft or, in fact, by the two combined."[24] Moreover, over a twenty-five year period from 1970 to 1995, ServiceMaster provided a return to its shareholders of 25 percent compounded annually, more twice double the return achieved by the stock market during this period.[25] From the mid-1970s to the mid-1990s, this firm ranked number one among the *Fortune* 1000 in terms of its return on investment.[26]

Beyond profitability, business organizations, my research indicates, led by executives with a strong evangelical faith have an advantage in the current business climate. These firms generally show high levels of employee customer satisfaction as well as outstanding products or services. However, they have a mixed record with respect to the environment.

From a corporate governance viewpoint, I conclude that it is difficult, but not impossible, to maintain a unique corporate culture, specifically, an evangelical Christian-orientation, after a firm goes public or as it grows larger. It is far easier for a founder, such as David R. Parker of Covenant Transport and R. B. Pamplin, Jr. of the Pamplin Corp., to formulate and maintain, rather than to change, an organization's culture. However, organizational transformation is possible as demonstrated by Norm Miller at Interstate Batteries, John D. Beckett at Beckett Corp., both privately held corporations, and Ken Melrose, at Toro, a publicly held concern. As we will see with ServiceMaster and Herman Miller, however, it is not easy to maintain an organization's historic approach, especially in a publicly held corporation, if leadership passes to financially oriented executives focused on striving to increase shareholder value.

Publicly held businesses present special challenges for CEOs wishing to assert their religious faith and values in a corporate context. Shareholders and investors assert that their interests are paramount. Unless a founder maintains a controlling share interest, for example, David R. Parker of Covenant Transport, public corporations generally find it harder to remain true to corporate missions and core values that consider other stakeholder (non-shareholder) interests. However, it is not impossible, as demonstrated by Ken Melrose of Toro, to implement and maintain a biblically based, stewardship or servant-leadership style (or mix of both) and create an accompanying corporate culture. Privately controlled firms, such as Pamplin, Interstate Batteries, and Beckett particularly, the latter two, both relatively small corporations, in terms of numbers of personnel, offer CEOs far more latitude in creating and maintaining a distinct, values-based corporate identity and the ability to keep out strong dissenters as top executives and managers.

As a firm grows and becomes more complex, more layers separate leaders from followers, making it increasingly difficult for employees to embrace and implement a distinctive corporate mission and core values. With more personnel, come divergent backgrounds and viewpoints and thus the trend, as exemplified by ServiceMaster, for larger business entities to become more inclusive, giving space for everyone.A word or two is in order regarding what this book is not about. It does not deal with the broad topic of business ethics. (Parenthetically, I note that the Sarbanes-Oxley Act of 2002 requires each publicly held reporting company to disclose whether it has adopted a code of ethics for its senior financial officers.[27] It is not about Americans trying to forge a stronger connection between their religious (or spiritual) lives and the workplace. It does not consider the conflict between a Friday-Saturday-Sunday religious commitment to be loving, compassionate, caring and generous and the weekday behavior found in competitive, high-pressure jobs and organizations. It is not about the bubbling up from the bottom as employees respond to this divide between their religious (or spiritual) values and their work. It does not consider the burgeoning trend to the formation of Bible and prayer groups that meet regularly in the workplace, the quest for personal observance of religious customs in the workplace, or the use of meditation and other spiritual disciplines to cope with stress.[28] It omits any discussion regarding the legalities of individuals (or groups of employees) striving to express their religion (or spirituality) at work through: requests for space in conference rooms and other work locations and time for religious observance (prayer or meditation), study, or discussion during work breaks; the formation of groups to discuss religious (or spiritual) topics, wanting to display religious materials in the workplace (such as, hanging a cross on a computer or placing a scriptural book near the telephone), or wearing religious symbols or dress at work. Suffice it to say that federal civil rights legislation offers employees broad religious protection, requiring private sector businesses engaged in interstate commerce, with fifteen or more employees for each workday in each twenty or more calendar weeks during the current or previous calendar year, to accommodate on-the-job religious observance and practice within "reasonable" limits.[29] Thus, those employers covered by federal rules and regulations must make "reasonable accommodation" for their employees' religious needs, such as time off for religious observances or requests to display of religious materials in the workplace, wear religious symbols, and provide space or time for religious observance, study, or discussion during work breaks. However, courts do not allow one employee to create a hostile work environment for others by harassing them about what they do (or do not believe).

Rather, I want to focus on an entire corporation's culture and its goals and achievements through the leadership provided by those at the top of an organization. In short, I will examine a small number of companies that have set off on one particular religious journey, evangelical Christianity, where a founder or a chief executive officer either leads according to this faith approach or uses this path as the focus of a firm's mission and core values thereby striving to unify its employees around a common purpose.

Notes

1.   Andrew S. Grove, "Stigmatizing Business," *Washington Post*, July 17, 2002, A 23.
2.   Testimony of Alan Greenspan, chairman, Board of Governors, Federal Reserve System, "Monetary Policy Report," *Oversight Hearing on the Federal Reserve's Second Monetary Policy Report to Congress for 2002*, U.S. Congress, Senate Banking, Housing and Urban Affairs Committee, 107th Congress 2nd Session (July 16, 2002), 5; *New York Times*, "Excerpts From Report By Greenspan at Senate," July 17, 2002, C8. Matt Murray, "Options Frenzy: What Went Wrong?, *Wall Street Journal*, December 17, 2002, B1, examines the negative impact of stock options.

3. Robert L. Bartley, "Risk Aversion in the Corner Office," *Wall Street Journal*, December 2, 2002, A19.
4. Adolf A. Berle, Jr., "Corporate Powers as Powers in Trust," *Harvard Law Review* 44:7 (May 1931): 1049-1074, at 1049.
5. E. Merrick Dodd, Jr., "For Whom are Corporate Managers Trustees?," *Harvard Law Review* 45:7 (May 8, 1932): 1144-1163, at 1148.
6. Adolph A. Berle, Jr., "Foreword," to *The Corporation in Modern Society*, ed. Edward S. Mason (Cambridge, MA: Harvard University 1960), xii.
7. Milton Friedman with Rose D. Friedman, *Capitalism and Freedom* (Chicago: University of Chicago, 1962), 133.
8. Milton Friedman, "The Social Responsibility of Business Is to Increase Its Profits," *New York Times Magazine*, September 13, 1970, 32 - 33, 122, 124, 126, at 33, reprinted in *Ethical Issues In Business: A Philosophical Approach*, eds. Thomas Donaldson and Patricia H. Werhane (Englewood Cliffs, NJ: Prentice-Hall, 1980), 191-197.
9. *A.P. Smith Manufacturing Co. v Barlow*, 98 A2d 581 (NJ 1953), appeal dismissed, 346 US 861 (1953).
10. *Theodore Holding Corp. v Henderson*, 257 A2d 398 (Del Ch 1969).
11. American Law Institute, *Principles of Corporate Governance: Analysis and Recommendations*, volume 1, Parts I-VI (St. Paul, MN: American Law Institute, 1994), 55 (§ 2.01 The Objective and Conduct of the Corporation). The comments to Section 2.01 dealing with the economic objective, ethical considerations, as well as public welfare, humanitarian, educational, philanthropic purposes, amplify the approach of these principles. Ibid., 57-60, 62-69 (§ 2.01, Comments f. The economic objective, h. Ethical considerations, i. Public welfare, humanitarian, educational, and philanthropic purposes).
12. Charles Colson, "Law Isn't Enough," *Washington Post*, July 30, 2002, A17.
13. John D. Beckett, Chairman and CEO, R.W. Beckett Corp., iPriority, Special Edition, available at http://www.ipriority.com/america/html/beckett/h.
14. John D. Beckett, "Noble Ideas for Business," *Management Review* 88:3 (March 1999):62.
15. Lewis D. Solomon, *A Modern Day Rabbi's Interpretation of the Teachings of Jesus* (Pittsburgh, PA: CeShore, 2000); Lewis D. Solomon, "Jesus: A Prophet of Universalistic Judaism," in *Jesus Through Jewish Eyes: Rabbis and Scholars Engage an Ancient Brother in a New Conversation*, ed. Beatrice Bruteau (Maryknoll, NY: Orbis Books, 2001).
16. Laura L. Nash, *Believers in Business* (Nashville, TN: Thomas Nelson, 1994), 46.
17. Ibid., 272.
18. Ibid., 48.
19. Brian J. Zinnbauer et al., "Religion and Spirituality: Unfuzzying the Fuzzy," *Journal For the Scientific Study of Religion* 36:4 (December 1997): 549-564.
20. Ian I. Mitroff and Elizabeth A. Denton, *A Spiritual Audit of Corporate America: A Hard Look At Spirituality, Values, and Religion in the Workplace* (San Francisco, CA: Jossey-Bass, 1999), 67.
21. Ibid., at 15-27; Kenneth I. Pargament and Annette Mahoney, "Spirituality: Discovering and Conserving the Sacred" in *Handbook of Positive Psychology*, eds. C.R. Snyder and Shane J. Lopez, (New York: Oxford University, 2002); Ian I. Mitroff and Elizabeth A. Denton, "A Study of Spirituality in the Workplace," *Sloan Management Review* 40:4 (Summer 1999): 83-92, at 88-89.
22. Rushwood M. Kidder, "Universal Human Values: Finding an Ethical Common Ground," *Futurist* 28:4 (July/August 1994): 8-13, reprinted in *The Leader's Com-

panion: Insights on Leadership Through the Ages, ed. J. Thomas Wren (New York: The Free Press, 1995), 500-508.

23. John D. Beckett, *Loving Monday: Succeeding in Business Without Selling Your Soul* (Downers Grove, IL: InterVarsity, 1998), 91.

24. Jeffrey Pfeffer, *The Human Equation: Building Profits By Putting People First* (Boston, MA: Harvard Business School, 1998), 7.

25. Ibid., 297. See also Noel M. Tichy with Eli Cohen, *The Leadership Engine: How Winning Companies Build Leaders at Every Level* (New York: HarperBusiness, 1997), 13.

26. James L. Heskett, *ServiceMaster: We Serve,* Harvard Business School Case N9-900-030, Boston, MA (June 6, 2000), 2.

27. Section 406, Title IV, Public Law No. 107-204, 116 Statutes-at-Large 789 (2002), 15 USC § 7264. Section 7264(c) defines a "code of ethics" as "such standards as are reasonably necessary to promote—(1) honest and ethical conduct, including the ethical handling of actual or apparent conflicts of interest between personal and professional relationships; (2) full, fair, accurate, timely, and understandable disclosure in the periodic reports required to be filed by the issuer; and (3) compliance with applicable governmental rules and regulations. Furthermore, rules of the U.S. Securities and Exchange Commission, 17 Code of Federal Regulations § 228.406, now mandate that publicly held reporting companies disclose in their annual reports to shareholders, whether they have adopted a written code of ethics for their principal executive officers or principal financial officers, among others, and if not, why not. See also Steven Savides, "Firms Raise Their Own Code of Ethics," *Christian Science Monitor,* November 4, 2002, 18; Raphael S. Grunfeld, "Enforcing a Written Code of Ethics," *New York Law Journal,* November 18, 2002, S3.

28. See, e.g., Michelle Conlin, "Religion in the Workplace," *Business Week* 3653 (November 1, 1999): 150-158; Timothy D. Schellhardt, "In a Factory Schedule, Where Does Religion Fit In?", *Wall Street Journal,* March 4, 1999, B1; Caryle Murphy, "Workers Taking Religion to the Office," *Washington Post,* September 12, 1998, B1; Abraham McLaughlin, "Seeking Spirituality...At Work," *Christian Science Monitor,* March 16, 1998, 1.

29. 42 USC §2000e (b) and (j). 29 Code of Federal Regulations §1605.2 construe the phrase "reasonable accommodation without undue hardship."

2

Who are the Evangelical Business Executives and What are Their Leadership Styles?

This book focuses on firms headed by evangelical Christians. Some have a private faith; others want their faith to shine forth. After briefly offering an example of those CEOs who take a low-key approach in a corporate context, this chapter examines the leadership styles of two groups of evangelical executives. One group, the preachers, weaves their religious faith into the fabric of their businesses. They want to proselytize non-believers, including employees, customers, and suppliers. Another group, taking a more sophisticated approach, based on the biblical principles of stewardship or servanthood (or both), actively pursues a values-management strategy. Before considering how these executives seek to align their work and business with their religious faith and values, it is helpful to consider evangelicalism in American and provide some statistical data on evangelical executives.

Evangelical Christianity in the United States and Its Impact of Business Executives

Evangelicalism emerged in America in the eighteenth century, during the First Great Awakening, "as virtually a new form of Protestantism, one centered in the experience and affairs of the individual believer as opposed to the teaching and worship of the church."[1] Evangelicalism stressed not only the conversion of non-believers and holy living but also encouraged believers, building on the momentum from the Second Great Awakening, beginning in the early part of the nineteenth century, especially during the 1820s and 1830s, to create a society reflecting Christian mores. Nineteenth-century evangelicals opposed slavery (at least in the North), Sab-

17

bath-breaking, and alcohol. They sought to help those in need. By the last decade of the nineteenth century, most American Protestants were evangelicals.

By the 1920s, however, American Protestants lost their unifying force. Traditionalists remained committed to the authority of the Bible. Liberal Protestants sought an accommodation to the challenges posed by science. As liberals captured mainline Protestant churches, evangelicals found themselves at the margins of Protestant American. Between 1920 and 1960, evangelicals, during a time of retrenchment, attained a distinct religious identity. Beginning in the 1960s evangelicals engaged culture and politics in response to well-known secularizing trends. In addition to striving to protect the nuclear family with traditional gender roles and responsibilities, evangelicals sought the adoption of conservative social policies through political action.

By the late 1960s, mainstream Protestant churches began to witness a decline in membership, with evangelical denominations growing in number. Recent estimates place the number of evangelical Christians as high as forty to forty-six percent of the U.S. population.[2] Exact figures are not available because evangelical Christians maintain loose denominational affiliations, ranging beyond traditional religious structures. As one expert on evangelical Protestantism in the United States stated, "Part of the problem [in understanding evangelicalism] is the movement's lack of boundaries or formal status. No single denomination claims to be the Evangelical Church of America."[3]

As a result, statistics on evangelical executives are hard to come by for one major reason. There is no generally agreed upon, single definition of evangelical Christianity.[4] As noted, evangelicals are diverse in terms of denominational affiliations. Most, but not all, evangelicals have been "born again." They have experienced some type of "conversion" (or "reconversion") resulting from the development of a personal relationship with Jesus and a specific commitment (or re-commitment) to Him as the criterion for entering heaven. They generally assume a responsibility to bear witness to and invite others to receive Jesus, thereby changing other's lives through individual conversions. They are, however, divided on Bible inerrancy, namely, whether to read the Bible literally and whether the Bible is the infallible word of God. Many see all aspects of human existence as subject to biblical authority. These believers see the practicality of the Bible, which they hold in high regard as God's revelation to humanity. Beyond church attendance, many, but not all, seek to practice their faith in all realms of their lives. Marion E. Wade, the founder of ServiceMaster, bluntly stated, "If you don't live it [your religious faith], you don't believe it."[5]

Since World War II, evangelicals, a leading academic noted, "have been extremely unrepresented among the top leadership of America's large corporations, which mainline Protestantism has dominated. As a group, evangelicals have been among those with the worst economic performance in America."[6] However, one study indicates that nearly one half of U.S. "small" business owners identify themselves as born-again Christians.[7] Others indicate that evangelicals comprise 43 percent of all U.S. business executives.[8]

Many of these evangelical business founders and chief executive officers wish to use their organizations to spread the message about Jesus.[9] They want to witness and to impart, in some way, with others, including their employees, customers, suppliers, and the community, how a personal relationship with God and Jesus, particularly the latter, changed their lives.

Regardless of their approach, low key, preacher, or more sophisticated, these executives, as good evangelists, want to share with a wider audience, as John D. Beckett, chairman and chief executive officer of R.W. Beckett Corp. put it, how the "personal and vital relationship with Jesus Christ...has transformed" his life.[10]

A Low-Key Approach to Evangelism

Some evangelical executives take a low key, non-preaching approach. Those in this category do not directly impose their religious views on their employees or expose these views to their customers or suppliers. They draw clear lines between their religious faith and their business. They do not impose their religious views on their corporations and its stakeholders; they do not preach at the office, openly discuss their faith, or sponsor company prayer groups, among activities others use to demonstrate their beliefs.

Jeffrey H. Coors, a daily Bible reader, and evangelical who attends a nondenominational Christian fellowship, serves as an example of this type of executive. For years, Coors struggled with how to integrate his faith and his work as he toiled, taking over his father and uncle's role as head of Adolph Coors Co. By 1985, he had become president of the family business which consisted of the beer business, a ceramics unit, and a variety of other commercial endeavors.

In 1989, after considerable prayer and discussion, Coors concluded that his business was his calling. It was where God wanted him to be. Discovering how to integrate his faith and his work, he found more inner peace "by being with God than doing for God." According to Coors, "It boils down to being the kind of person God created me to be.... Being the person He created me to be will bring Him glory and fulfill His original plan." Coors came to honor his relationship with God, making it a point to stay close to God, and then with the people God placed around him. For Coors, "It all boils down to respect and relationships with people. Respecting people is part of who I am. I hold people in ultimate respect, thank them for their contributions, and congratulate them for the successes. Sometimes it is simply being there for them when things don't go well."[11]

Coors left his family's firm in 1992 when it spun off its packaging, ceramics, aluminum, and developing technologies businesses to ACX Technologies, Inc. (ACX).[12] As a result of a series of acquisitions in 1998 and 1999, ACX became the leading folding carton manufacturer for consumer products in North America. In 1999, to focus on folding carton packaging, ACX sold its aluminum rigid container sheet business as well as its flexible packaging unit. In that year, ACX also spun off its ceramic, metal and plastic manufacturing components businesses into CoorsTek, Inc., which became a maker of critical components and assemblies for the semiconductor equipment industry and other business sectors. In May 2000, ACX changed its name to Graphic Packaging International Corp. and, subsequently, in 2003 merged with Riverwood Holding Co., the owner of Riverwood International Corp. a privately held maker of packaging. Coors served as chairman from 2000 to 2003 and chief executive officer and president from 1992 to 2003 of Graphic Packaging International, and as executive chairman of the merged companies, Graphic Packaging Corp., beginning in 2003.

Reflecting a low-key approach to evangelical Christianity and its application to the business world, Coors framed how he injected his religious faith and values into a publicly held corporation as follows:

> I like to stress a personal relationship with our heavenly father through Jesus Christ, because then you're just talking to a friend, and you get direction, understanding, and wisdom from a higher power. The problem with religion is that man gets things really

confused with all the rules and regulations and procedures, when the important thing is whether Christ is on the throne in your heart.

You can be good, righteous people in the workplace and conduct your affairs in a righteous manner without getting overly religious or threatening. But I'm very open about my faith with fellow employees. I regularly talk about the fact that we are created in God's image and that He has given us free will, but that our duty is to respect others. I encourage people to be all that God created, the best you can be. And I say that life consists of heavenly relationships and that the most important relationship in my life is with our heavenly father through his son Jesus Christ.

You can function perfectly well as a very upright company, obeying all the laws. In fact, I actually think you can prosper better as a company if God is your focal point.[13]

Corporate Executives as Preachers

Other executives, as preachers, weave their religious faith into the fabric of their businesses. They want others to accept the tenets of evangelical Christianity, specifically, to know and make a commitment to Jesus (in other words, to be born again) and live the virtues of a "Christ-honoring, selfless, forgiving spirit."[14] They strive, intensely and energetically, to demonstrate their "love for Christ in and through [their] work before [their] words will be heard. Decisive Christ-honoring action is needed."[15]

These enthusiastic, "buttonholing" executives, who wear their faith on their sleeves, actively proselytize others, thereby trying to save as many souls as possible. Sharing their approach to Christianity with nonbelievers, they offer one-on-one testimonials, assuming a responsibility to bear witness to Jesus and invite others to receive Him.

As overt witnesses wanting to introduce others to Jesus, they look to the New Testament, where Jesus said, "Whoever acknowledges me before men, I will also acknowledge him before my Father in heaven" (Matthew 10:32). When Jesus appeared to His disciples after the Resurrection, He told them: "Go into all the world and preach the good news to all creation." (Mark 16:15). They view Jesus as the way to God and salvation. As Jesus stated, "I am the way and the truth and the life. No one comes to the Father except through me." (John 14:6; Acts 4:12, 10:43). John D. Beckett put it, "The ultimate goal (and privilege) in life is to know God intimately—and this happens as we establish and maintain a personal relationship with Jesus Christ."[16]

They also look to Jesus imploring those who were listening to Him to take His message out into the surrounding world. Jesus stated:

"You are the salt of the earth. But if salt loses its saltiness, how can it be made salty again? It is no longer good for anything, except to be thrown out and trampled by men." (In ancient times, salt was not only an agent to create thirst, it also served as a preservative. In doing its job, salt could be an irritant). Jesus continued: "You are the light of the world. A city on a hill cannot be hidden. Neither do people light a lamp and put it under a bowl. Instead they put it on its stand, and it gives light to everyone in the house. In the same way, let your light shine before men, that they may see your good deeds and praise your Father in heaven" (Matthew 5:13-16).

Empirical evidence demonstrates the role of corporate executives as preachers. One study (n=152) of self-identified Christian (but not only evangelical Christian) companies, with at least fifteen employees, using questionnaires and follow up interviews with twenty-five firms, found that 92 percent (136) of these organizations engaged in regular, on-site religious activities.[17] These included preaching by CEOs, scriptural reading, personal witnessing, devotional time, inspirational talks, and opening meetings with prayers and Bible readings. These prayer groups may promote a greater sense of community and mutual accountability thereby preventing (or at least delaying) layoffs or the reduction in corporate benefit packages.[18] A large percentage (73 percent) actively proselytized their customers, regaling them with Christian books and paraphernalia as well as Christian conversations and witnessing.[19] They enclose biblical quotations in product materials (packaging, invoices, and stationery), distribute corporate brochures and literature with biblical materials, and invite them to their church to worship. About half (48 percent) also proselytize their suppliers.[20]

Many of these companies also demonstrated, it is important to add, the application of Christian religious values to the business world. Forty-nine percent of the firms surveyed (sixty-nine companies) stressed employee-centered values and actions, such as the Golden Rule, kindness, trust, integrity and cooperation. Many (45 percent or sixty-six businesses) emphasized the importance of product or service quality and customer satisfaction.[21]

Some of the evangelical executives profiled in this book, believing that their religious faith is the only true path to gaining salvation from an eternity in hell, more openly than the low-key approach of Coors, take on the role of preacher. They use their corporate position to intervene actively in others' lives in a personal way, focusing on their employees, customers, and sometimes their suppliers. Executives, such as David Parker of Covenant Transport, a number of CEOs at ServiceMaster, beginning with its founder, Marion Wade, and Norm Miller of Interstate Batteries, try to spread the good news. They interact with their employees like a minister as well as a boss. Their firm's product literature trumpets scripture. They openly display their companies' Christian identities.

A More Sophisticated Approach:
Stewardship and Servant-Leadership

Other evangelical executives take a more sophisticated approach to their religious faith and values in their business decisions and actions as well as in their relationships with their employees, customers, and suppliers. Their religious faith comes to permeate every aspect of their life, including business matters. In striving to see and implement a connection between their religious faith and their businesses, two values guide their actions: stewardship and servanthood.

Stewardship. Evangelical executives look to the lesson Jesus taught on stewardship in His parable on the talents, a unit of currency in that day. For those who are unfamiliar with this parable (Matthew 25:14-30; Luke 19:12-26), it is helpful to see how Jesus sought to encourage His followers to use fully their abilities:

> Again, it will be like a man going on a journey, who called his servants and entrusted his property to them. To one he gave five talents of money, to another two talents, and to another one talent, each according to his ability. Then he went on his journey. The man who had received the five talents went at once and put his money to work and gained five more. So also, the one with the two talents gained two more. But the man who had received the one talent went off, dug a hole in the ground and hid his master's money.
>
> After a long time the master of those servants returned and settled accounts with them. The man who had received the five talents brought the other five. "Master," he said, "you entrusted me with five talents. See, I have gained five more."
>
> His master replied, "Well done, good and faithful servant! You have been faithful with a few things; I will put you in charge of many things. Come and share your master's happiness!"
>
> The man with the two talents also came. "Master," he said, "You entrusted me with two talents; see, I have gained two more."
>
> His master replied, "Well done, good and faithful servant! You have been faithful with a few things; I will put you in charge of many things. Come and share your master's happiness!"
>
> Then the man who had received the one talent came. "Master," he said, "I knew that you are a hard man, harvesting where you have not sown and gathering where you have not scattered seed. So I was afraid and went out and hid your talent in the ground. See, here is what belongs to you."

His master replied, "You wicked, lazy servant! So you knew that I harvest where I have not sown and gather where I have not scattered seed? Well then, you should have put my money on deposit with the bankers, so that when I returned I would have received it back with interest."

"Take the talent from him and give it to the one who has the ten talents. For everyone who has will be given more, and he will have an abundance. Whoever does not have, even what he has will be taken from him. And throw that worthless servant outside, into the darkness, where there will be weeping and gnashing of teeth."

The teaching is broader than financial stewardship, traditionally, money and physical assets; it is even broader than its more recent embodiment, namely, stewardship of the earth and our environment. The talent represents a symbol of human abilities and opportunities. We are called to use the principle of stewardship, aptly described as holding "something in trust for another,"[22] to facilitate the development not only of one's own abilities, opportunities, and resources but also those of others, especially one's employees. As stewards, business executives ought to ponder the power and wealth entrusted to them and what they will pass on to future generations. We will see this in R.B. Pamplin, Jr.'s approach at the R.B. Pamplin Corp. In addition to corporate charitable giving by the Pamplin Corp., Herman Miller, Interstate Batteries, and Beckett Corp., as well as the environmental consciousness at Herman Miller, stewardship leads evangelical executives to focus on the preservation and enhancement of assets and the creation of an environment for the growth and development of an organization's people along with an emphasis on product quality and customer service.

Servanthood. The stewardship of various business relationships leads to the concept of being a servant, specifically, a servant-leader. Striving to implement the notion of servant hood represents a common goal among some evangelical executives. They seek to follow the example of Jesus, Who came to serve, not be served, by putting the interests of others above their own interests. They try to serve their employees who, in turn, serve their customers.

The concept of servant-leadership, genuinely putting others first, represents a powerful, values-driven leadership approach, especially for those who see it as biblically rooted. The New Testament records that a leader must serve others. Those executives who put on the mantle of servant hood demonstrate the enduring wisdom of Jesus' example. As Jesus stated, "Instead, whoever wants to be great among you must be your servant, and whoever wants to be first, must be the slave of all. For even the Son of Man did not come to be served, but to serve, and to give his life as a ransom for many" (Mark 10:43-45; Matthew 20:26-27). Jesus also taught, "The greatest among you will be your servant. For whoever exalts himself will be humbled, and whoever humbles himself will be exalted" (Matthew 23:11-12).

For evangelical executives the concept of servant hood comes from learning that Jesus washed the feet of His disciples, when they sat at a table with their dirty feet (John 13:4-17). After dinner was served, He "got up from the meal, took off his outer clothing and wrapped a towel around his waist. After that, he poured water into a basin and he began to wash his disciples' feet, drying them with the towel that was wrapped around [H]im" (John 13:4-5). As Jesus stated: "Now that I, your Lord and Teacher, have washed your feet, you should also wash one another's feet. I have set you an example that you should do as I have done for you" (John 13:14-15). In the first century, people walked in sandals along dirty, dusty, muddy roads. Washing someone's feet, a demeaning task, was relegated to one's host's servant or in the absence of a servant, to the lowest-ranking guest. Jesus' action was a lesson in humility. It also served as an example of servant leadership, namely, one's power to choose to serve others.

Other New Testament writings indicate that Jesus represents the model of true servanthood. He came to serve, not to be served. As the Apostle Paul wrote of Jesus:

> Who, being in very nature God, did not consider equality with God something to be grasped, but made himself nothing, taking the very nature of a servant, being made in human likeness. And being found in appearance as a man, he humbled himself and became obedient to death—even death on a cross! (Paul's Letter to the Philippians 2:6-8)

Evangelical Christians see Jesus coming to the earth in humility. His servant nature manifested itself at His birth, where Mary placed Him in a manger, a feeding trough, for animals (Luke 2:7). Living modestly, He gave to others lavishly, continually. After His death on the Cross, a crude form of execution, His early followers lived out His example. They understood the benefit of serving and extending themselves on behalf of others. Today, the followers of Jesus strive to serve others.

The notion of servant-leadership received a powerful boost from the writings of Robert K. Greenleaf, a Quaker, who in turn, influenced a generation of evangelical executives, especially orienting them to a personalized approach to exercising power and to valuing and deeply caring for their employees, at all levels in an organization. We will see Greenleaf's impact on executives at ServiceMaster and Herman Miller. Max DePree, the former CEO of Herman Miller, noted that the "finest instruction" in how to practice the servant hood of leadership is found in Greenleaf's book, *Servant Leadership*.[23]

As a pragmatic idealist, Greenleaf focused in getting things done, while helping people grow. He spent his first career at AT&T Corp., mostly in human resources; when he retired in 1964, he was director of management research. At age sixty, he started another career, setting up the Center for Applied Ethics, a small think tank, since renamed the Robert K. Greenleaf Center for Servant Leadership. For Greenleaf, true leadership emerges from a primary motivation, a deep desire to help others.

Greenleaf coined the phrase "servant-leader" as a way of being in relationship with others. Bringing together the words "servant" and "leader" in a meaningful way, Greenleaf saw a servant-leader as one who is a servant first; one who strives to serve other's needs. A servant-leader shares mistakes and pain; he or she is self-effacing and humble, no matter how exalted one's position in the corporate hierarchy or the extent of the revenues (and profits) of one's organization.

Some of the traits of an executive as a servant-leader flow from deeply held beliefs about the persons, their dignity and worth. According to Greenleaf, the servant-leader takes his or her employees seriously. He or she recognizes that humans have a value in their own right. He or she tries to bring out the best in one's employees, whether office or factory workers or service personnel, by assuming responsibility for their growth and development and through their empowerment. In other words, for a servant-leader, a business exists, in part, to provide people with meaningful work so that they might experience their work as fulfilling, thereby realizing their potential. According to Greenleaf, "The work exists for the person as much as the person exists for the work. Put another way, the business exists as much to provide meaningful work to the person as it exists to provide a product or service to the customer."[24] Thus, work ought to offer an opportunity for emotional fulfillment and the nurturing of the human potential.

Greenleaf came to advocate a new leadership model, one placing serving others, including employees, customers, and community, an executive's number one priority. As he wrote:

The servant-leader is servant first....It beings with the natural feeling that one wants to serve, to serve first. Then conscious choice brings one to aspire to lead. That person is sharply different from one who is leader first....

The difference manifests itself in the care taken by the servant-first to make sure that other people's highest priority needs are being served....Do those served grow as persons? Do they, while being served, become healthier, wiser, freer, more autonomous, more likely themselves to become servants?[25]

In responding to the question: what business are you in?, a CEO as servant-leader, according to Greenleaf, will answer:

I am in the business of growing people—people who are stronger, healthier, more autonomous, more self-reliant, more competent. Incidentally, we also make and sell at a profit things that people want to buy so we can pay for all this. We play that game hard and well and we are successful the usual standards, but that is really incidental....We simply changed our aim....Consequently, as an institution, we are terribly strong. In fact, we are distinguished. How do I know we are distinguished? We select the best of the best and, once inside, then never want to leave. Any business that can do that is a winner.[26]

Thus, the servant-leader not only enhances the personal growth and development of a firm's employees, through a holistic approach to work, he or she also strives to improve the quality of organizational life. Based on the caring behavior of top executives, the servant-leader seeks to involve others in decision-making, at least at some level, by shifting responsibility downward. A CEO following this approach also helps to develop future servant-leaders and, more generally, enabling others to become more than they ever believed possible.

Although never reduced to a list by Greenleaf, one commentator formulated ten characteristics that connote a servant-leader as follows:

1. Listening to others and striving to identify and clarify the will of a group;

2. Empathy, accepting and recognizing people for their special and unique gifts;

3. Healing oneself and one's relationship to others and making broken spirits whole:

4. Awareness, being sharply aware about oneself and general conditions, leads to viewing most situations from a more holistic situation.

5. Persuasion, seeking to convince, not coerce compliance or use one's positional authority, and striving to build consensus.

6. Conceptualization, the ability to dream great dreams, by broad-based conceptual thinking;

7. Foresight, the ability to understand lessons from the past, see the realities of the present, and the likely consequences of any decision for the future;

8. Stewardship, as previously mentioned, the sense of holding something in trust for another;

9. Commitment to the growth of each and every employee based on a belief that people have an intrinsic value beyond their tangible contributions as workers;

10. Building community among those who work within an organization.[27]

Stepping back from the religious value of servant hood and its secular exposition, in carefully researched study of evangelical Protestant business executives, based on interviews with sixty-five CEOs, heads of successful firms, who were admired for their ethics, Laura L. Nash, a business ethicist at Harvard Business School, offered several interesting conclusions, focusing on the impact of their religious faith from a strategic business standpoint. She saw that many of these executives adroitly blended Christian values and a quest for profits.

Nash noted a commitment by her interviewees to what they regarded as the "Christian concept" of high quality goods and services[28] and to what she called employee "dignification."[29] In practical terms, dignification, based on the love of one's neighbor, meant the respect for one another. Many of these executives viewed employee-oriented efforts aimed at empowerment and the promotion of employees' dignity as a key to their business success. As nurturers and empowerers of human potential, these CEOs focused their stewardship on their employees' lives,[30] perhaps in a somewhat paternalistic manner. Nurturing of others led to exemplary treatment of their employees. It often took the form of providing their personnel with opportunities to develop the skills requisite to accomplishing their jobs through extensive investment in employee training and development.[31]

Nash also focused on these executives' "relational thinking," namely, the creation of mutually enabling relationships and the encouragement of employees to meaningfully relate to each other and a firm's customers.[32] The emphasis of relationships led to the existence of a strong, egalitarian attitude characterized by: a prevalence of participatory work forces; team-oriented decision-making; and an openness in communications.[33] By serving their employees, these business leaders sought to channel individual needs into productive harmony with group needs so as to fulfill the entity's purpose, namely, efficiency and profitability.[34]

The executives Nash interviewed also saw business as a service, based on enabling relationships, thereby creating value for others. This orientation led to a focus on customer interests and the creation and maintenance of beneficial relationships with customers, among other stakeholders, through personal attention and providing high quality goods and services.[35]

True leadership, for servant-leaders, emerges from a primary motivation, namely, a profound, but genuine, desire to help and nurture others that manifests itself in a number of ways. Some evangelical executives, particularly those at ServiceMaster, demonstrate servant-leadership, in striving to enhance their employees' skills base, trying to respect every employee and enhance their dignity, and in working side-by-side with their employees. At Herman Miller, under the egalitarian policies implemented by the DePree family, particularly, the humility, approachability, and caring manifested by these executives, servant-leadership facilitated an environment where employees came to trust one another and top managers. John Beckett's employee-oriented practices at the Beckett Corp., promote human dignity and provide opportunities for employees to develop their skills. Thus, these sophisticated practitioners of their faith evidence genuine religious values in business matters. They sought to attract and retain employees who feel strongly committed to their organizations and promote customer satisfaction.

The policies and practices implemented many of the evangelical executives Nash surveyed (and some of those I will examine in this book) with respect to their employees conform to and coincide with the best practices of modern secular corporate managers, namely, "the importance of their people to their basic strategy and their success."[36] These people-oriented executives do not view their employees as costs to be reduced, but rather as intelligent, motivated, trustworthy individuals, an organization's most important and strategic asset.

Jeffrey Pfeffer, a Stanford Graduate School of Business professor, in his book, *The Human Equation*, developed seven practices of successful, high performance organizational arrangements that produce profits with and through people. The seven practices identified by Pfeffer are as follows:

First, employment security, that is, never having a layoff or furlough to adjust for economic downturns or the strategic errors of senior executives. This approach enables a firm to be an employer of choice by generating a sense of trust that produces higher levels of effort.

Second, selective hiring of new employees who will fit the organization's culture.

Third, the reorganization of work with self-managed teams and decentralized decision-making thereby enabling better trained, more skilled people to implement their knowledge.

Fourth, compensation contingent on organizational performance, including profit sharing and stock ownership, that rewards outstanding performance.

Fifth, extensive training to develop a skilled, highly motivated workforce having the knowledge and capability to perform the required tasks, a key strategic means to achieve enhanced productivity and customer service benefits, as well as the ability to work in teams.

Sixth, reduced status difference, for example, in wages and office arrangements.

Seventh, the sharing of information on financial and operating performance strategy, making certain employees know how to use this in decision-making coupled with access to top executives, thereby conveying a sense of trust to an organization's employees.[37]

According to Pfeffer, this multifaceted, people-based strategy achieves a number of positive performance results, including innovation, flexibility, customer service, productivity, cost reduction, skill development, which in turn, contribute to sustained competitive success and profitability.[38]

*   *   *

Let us start by seeing how evangelical executives promote their religious faith and values in and through their businesses by examining two corporations, Covenant Transport, Inc. and R.B. Pamplin Corp., whose leaders have consistently guided their firms in a specific direction.

Notes

1. D.G. Hart, *That Old-Time Religion in Modern America: Evangelical Protestantism in the Twentieth Century* (Chicago: Ivan R. Dee, 2002), 8. In this summary, I have drawn on the Hart, *Old-Time Religion*; Robert H. Kraphol and Charles H. Lippy, *The Evangelicals: A Historical, Thematic, and Biographical Guide* (Westport, CT: Greenwood, 1999), 3-90; Mark A. Noll, *American Evangelical Christianity: An Introduction* (Malden, MA: Blackwell, 2001), 9-28; Robert William Fogel, *The Fourth Great Awakening & the Future of Egalitarianism* (Chicago: University of Chicago, 2000), 19-28.
2. Randall Balmer, *Encyclopedia of Evangelicalism* (Louisville, KY: Westminster John Knox, 2002), 197. See also Laurie Goodstein, "Conservative Churches Grew Fastest in the 1990's Report Says," *New York Times*, September 18, 2002, A16.
3. Hart, *Old-Time Religion*, 201.
4. Laura L. Nash, *Believers in Business* (Nashville, TN: Thomas Nelson, 1994), 2-6; Balmer, *Encyclopedia*, 197; Noll, *Evangelicals*, 56-66.
5. Marion E. Wade with Glenn D. Kittler, *The Lord Is My Counsel: A Businessman's Personal Experiences with the Bible* (Englewood Cliffs, NJ: Prentice-Hall, 1966), 7.
6. Nash, *Believers*, 20.
7. Dan McGraw, "The Christian Capitalists," *U.S. News & World Report* 118:10 (March 13, 1995): 52-62, at 54.
8. Robert Darden and P.J. Richardson, *Corporate Giants: Personal Stories of Faith and Finance* (Grand Rapids, MI: Fleming H. Revell, 2002), 14.
9. Nash, *Believers*, 4-5.
10. Jim Braham, "The Spiritual Side," *Industry Week* 243:3 (February 1, 1999): 48-56, at 48.
11. The quotations in this paragraph are from Larry Julian, *God Is My CEO: Following God's Principles in a Bottom-Line World* (Avon, MA: Adams Media, 2002), 96-99.
12. I have drawn on Graphic Packaging International Corp. (GPIC), U.S. Securities and Exchange Commission (SEC) Form 10-K For the Fiscal Year Ended December 31, 2002 (March 24, 2003), 3, 16; GPIC, SEC Form 10K/A For the Fiscal Year Ended December 31, 2001 (July 30, 2002), 3, 19; GPIC, SEC Form 10-K For the Fiscal Year Ended December 31, 2000 (March 23, 2001), 3-9; CoorsTek, Inc. (CoorsTek), SEC Form 10-K For the Fiscal Year Ended December 31, 2001 (March 1, 2002), 2-4, 24; CoorsTek, SEC Form 10-K For the Fiscal Year Ended December 31, 1999 (March 30, 2000), 1-3; *New York Times*, "Riverwood Holding to Buy Graphic Packaging, A Rival," March 27, 2003, C4; Louis Aguilar, "Graphic Packaging Merger Set," *Denver Post*, March 27, 2003, C1. Also in 2003, CoorsTek was merged into a Coors' family company, Keystone Acquisition Corp. *New York Times*, "CoorsTek Accepts Pact With Coors Family," December 24, 2002, C3; *Wall Street Journal*," CoorsTek Inc.: Buyout by Coors Family Trust Is Agreed to at $215.8 Million, December 24, 2002, D2; Roger Fillion, "CoorsTek Leaves Wall Street," *Rocky Mountain News*, March 19, 2003, 4B.
13. Jim Braham, "Spiritual Side," at 56.
14. William Nix, *Transforming Your Workplace for Christ* (Nashville, TN: Broadman & Holman, 1997), 47.
15. Ibid., 195-196.
16. John Beckett, *Loving Monday: Succeeding in Business Without Selling Your Soul* (Downers Grove, IL: InterVarsity Press, 1998), 165.
17. Nabil A. Ibrahim et al., "Characteristics and Practices of 'Christian-Based' Companies," *Journal of Business Ethics* 10:2 (February 1991): 123-132, at 126.

18. Majia Holmer Nadesan, "The Discourses of Corporate Spiritualism and Evangelical Capitalism," *Management Communication Quarterly* 13:1 (August 1999): 3-42, at 31.
19. Ibrahim, "Characteristics," 128.
20. Ibid., at 130.
21. Ibid., at 127.
22. Peter Block, *Stewardship: Choosing Service Over Self-Interest* (San Francisco, CA: Berrett-Koehler, 1993), xx.
23. Max DePree, *Leadership Jazz* (New York: Dell, 1992), 10-11; Max DePree, *Leadership Is an Art* (New York: Dell, 1989), 12.
24. Robert K. Greenleaf, *Servant Leadership: A Journey into the Nature of Legitimate Power & Greatness* (Mahwah, NJ: Paulist Press, 1977), 154-155 (italics omitted).
25. Ibid., 27 (italics omitted).
26. Ibid., 159-160 (italics omitted).
27. Larry C. Spears, "Tracing the Growing Impact of Servant-Leadership," in *Insights on Leadership: Service, Stewardship, Spirit, and Servant-Leadership,* ed. Larry C. Spears (New York: John Wiley, 1998), 3-6. See also, Walter Kiechel III, "The Leader as Servant," *Fortune* 125:9 (May 4, 1992): 121-122.
28. Nash, *Believers*, 76.
29. Ibid., 131-134.
30. Ibid, 132.
31. Ibid., 131.
32. Ibid., 97, 123, 135-137, 271.
33. Ibid., 140-152.
34. Ibid., 133.
35. Ibid., 96-97.
36. Jeffery Pfeffer, *The Human Equation: Building Profits By Putting People First* (Boston: Harvard Business School, 1998), 294.
37. Ibid., 64-98. See also Jeffrey Pfeffer, "Seven Practices of Successful Organizations," *California Management Review* 40:2 (Winter 1998): 96-125.
38. Pfeffer, *Human Equation*, 301.

3

Covenant Transport, Inc.: A Religious-Based Corporation Led by a Preacher-Leader

The publicly held Covenant Transport, Inc. exemplifies a firm headed by an evangelical Christian that has consistently demonstrated a religious orientation. It represents those corporations with a constant religious-based presence that in many ways defines their existence. David R. Parker, the founder and head of Covenant Transport, is a preacher-leader. The firm manifests Parker's evangelical style to its employees and customers. Its employees see Parker's (and therefore, Covenant's) religious orientation in prayer meetings, Bible study groups, and through ministers who perform a variety of functions, including serving as corporate chaplains. Customers and the public-at-large also see the firm's religious beliefs.

Business Background

David R. Parker, an evangelical Christian, is the founder of Covenant Transport, Inc. and its president since the company's establishment in 1985. He has also served as the firm's chief executive officer and chairman of its board of directors since 1994.

After graduating from high school at age sixteen, Parker worked in his parents' (actually, his stepfather Clyde M. Fuller's) trucking business, Southwest Motor Freight, for the next eight years. He served in every department at that firm's corporate offices in Chattanooga, Tennessee, becoming vice president of operations and vice president of marketing. With two other employees, he ran the company's day-to-day operations.[1]

In 1985, Parker founded Covenant Transport as a long-haul, full truckload carrier, specializing in the time-sensitive delivery of retail merchandise and manufactured products for customers throughout the United States. Parker and his wife started the firm "with the objective of providing superior service to customers, while striving for honesty and integrity in relationships with customers, suppliers, drivers and employees."[2]

Covenant commenced business with twenty-five tractors and fifty trailers. In its first year of operation (1986), the firm generated $7.4 million of revenues. By early 1988, the company had expanded its fleet to about 150 tractors and during that year recorded $19.4 million in revenues.

In 1989, Parker wanted to buy a new building for Covenant Transport's corporate offices. He decided to keep seventy-five of the firm's tractors for eleven more months and use the projected equity of some $500,000 in these vehicles to pay for the headquarters building. Coming off of warranty, the tractors quickly deteriorated, however. Maintenance costs skyrocketed and Parker decided to sell them. Because of the high sales of new tractors and an overload of used tractors on the market, it took him most of 1989 to sell the vehicles. With maintenance plants at full capacity, he could not find a facility to recondition the tractors for several months. This delay resulted in additional maintenance expenses of $600,000. Because many tractors broke down at the same time, the firm experienced a decline in revenues and operating losses in 1989 and 1990.[3]

The 1990s brought prosperity to Covenant. Beginning in the fourth quarter of 1990, it eliminated its short- and medium-haul operations, focusing instead on providing time-sensitive transcontinental, express service.[4] The debts incurred in the late 1980s were reduced to a manageable level. The firm went public in 1994, raising $50.9 million, using all of the net proceeds to repay most of its secured debt, then totaling in excess of $65 million.[5] Today, Parker and his wife, Jacqueline, own over 45 percent of Covenant's voting stock and thus they constitute the firm's controlling shareholders.[6]

Revenues grew as a result of nine acquisitions from 1996 to 2001 and the internal expansion of its fleet and its customer base. As a nonunionized carrier, it picked off business with its lower cost, more flexible work force. By 2001, Covenant's revenues exceeded $547 million, but the firm recorded a net loss of $6.7 million that year (including a one-time pretax impairment charge of $15.4 million related to the reduced market value of its used tractors), a sharp decline in its operating income that reached over $43 million in 1999. However, in 2002, its net income rebounded to $8.3 million, although its revenues declined slightly to $542 million. As the seventh largest truckload carrier in the United States (and the fifth largest publicly held truckload carrier), it operated about 3,700 tractors and 7,500 trailers at the end of 2002.[7]

To provide expedited deliveries, generally over distances from 1,500 to 2,500 miles on many of its routes, Covenant uses two-person driver teams who alternate driving responsibility.[8] Although reducing the number of driver teams in 2001 and 2002 to better match the demand for long-haul service, teams currently operate about thirty percent of the company's vehicles.[9] Teams allow the firm to provide expedited service because they are able to handle longer routes and drive more miles yet stay within the U.S. Department of Transportation safety rules. However, teams require higher salaries and recruiting costs than solo drivers, thereby increasing personnel costs as a percentage of revenues as well as the number of drivers the company must recruit.

In the late 1990s, whether through corporate vision, serendipity, or divine guidance, Covenant's operations evolved in three respects, protecting the firm somewhat from a decline in industry volume, the increased cost of its tractors (due to higher initial prices and lower used tractor values) and insurance claims as well as elevated fuel prices.[10] First, beginning in 1997, the firm's presence grew in shorter hauls. By 2001, the firm's overall length of haul had decreased from 1,700 miles to about 1,100 miles, sheltering Covenant somewhat from one of the hardest hit segments of the trucking industry, long-haul, during the 2001-2002 economic slowdown, marked by a massive number of long-haul carrier failures.

Second, during this period, its customer mix changed. Services to other transportation companies (including less than truckload shipments too small to fill up an entire trailer but too big for the parcel titans, air freight, and freight forwarders that assemble shipments, assuming responsibility for transportation from receipt to destination) as well as third party freight consolidators (that accept less than truckload shipments and then combine them for delivery in full truck shipments) became a larger part of Covenant's customer mix. Covenant came to move less than truckload freight between other carriers' terminals. The increase in this type of business proved beneficial because it allowed for the more predictable timing of shipments and a higher level of consistency and customer service.

Third, the type of freight carried also changed. Through acquisitions and internal growth from 1997 to 2002, the firm expanded its fleet of temperature controlled trailers fivefold from approximately 200 to about 1,200. With a reduced number of remaining participants in this segment of the industry, as a result of smaller refrigerated carriers exiting the business and the bankruptcy of several larger refrigerated carriers, Covenant Transport will be one of the most significant players when an economic turnaround occurs.

In all the various facets of the trucking industry in which it competes, Covenant Transport emphasizes customer service and reliability. With the motto "Always on Time," the firm regularly achieves a 99 percent on-time performance.[11] Focusing on detail in its quest to achieve a perfect on-time record of customer service, Parker noted:

It strictly becomes focus. Our operation is good at looking at every load, and our marketing department works in coordination with operations, where we load 7,000 loads a week. To give 99% performance, 1% is 70 loads that we will have a problem with making the transit time and it's really just focusing on that freight on a day-to-day basis. So we meet, and we look at the ones that did run late, and once they are late we deal with it as it is happening. But then, later on, we will sit down in management and we will look at those customers and those late loads, and investigate why they happened and what we could have done to change it, and we will find throughout the system that there is an area of vulnerability somewhere on a particular haul resulting in a late run. Then we will review our processes to hopefully correct the service. Maybe it's at one of our outside terminal locations, maybe it is the nighttime operations, maybe it's the maintenance department at one of our shops who we need to deal with, and if so we'll work with them to make sure that we are tracking the trucks from point A to point B in the timely manner that we've got to. So in one word, it's just "focus, focus, focus," focus to detail to make sure your give the service.[12]

The firm uses cutting-edge technological systems to increase its operating efficiency, reduce costs, promote economics of scale, and improve its customer service. The Qualcomm Omnitracs system, a satellite-based tracking and communications system, permits direct communication between Covenant's drivers and its fleet managers. This system regularly updates a tractor's position to permit the company and its shippers to locate freight shipments and accurately estimate pick-up and delivery times. Covenant Transport also uses the Sensortracs System to monitor engine idling time, speed, and other factors impacting on operating efficiency.[13]

Parker's Religious Orientation: His Covenant with God

Parker became a born again Christian at age thirteen, and currently belongs to a Pentecostal sect, City Church.[14] The Pentecostal movement coalesced in the first decade of the twentieth century. On January 1, 1901, a student at the Bethel Bible College in Topeka, Kansas began speaking in tongues, an ecstatic form of speech typically in a language unknown to the speaker and those around him or her. This experience, more technically known as glossolalia, was linked to the first Pentecost (recorded in Acts 2 of the New Testament), when the Holy Spirit filled early Christians. As the movement grew, it burst into public awareness during the 1906 Azusa Street Revival in Los Angeles and quickly spread thereafter. Today, most Pentecostals, including Parker, believe in speaking in tongues and other gifts of the Holy Spirit, including divine healing.[15]

Parker founded Covenant Transport in 1985 following a "precipitating crisis." After his parents sold their company in 1984, Parker remained with the firm, as a vice president, for eight months. He then resigned, feeling, as he later stated, "God was leading me in another direction."[16] He planned to start another trucking business with his two assistants, "even though a small, still voice inside me kept saying, 'No'." Parker continued:

> Soon there came a time when God started dealing with me. I developed a severe sleeping problem that lasted for several months. I would only sleep in naps of 10 or 15 minutes each. During one period I went 48 hours without any sleep.
>
> I became very emotionally and physically tired and began taking sleeping pills. I knew God could solve this problem for me, so I began quoting Scriptures and standing on His word. But nothing happened. You see, I refused to deal with the real problem in my life. I was going against God's will.[17]

Then Parker and one of his brother-in-law went on a religious retreat for several days. During this retreat he reached a covenant with God that led to founding of his own trucking company. He entered into a dialogue with God through prayer. Parker saw that any barriers to succeed would be removed once he gave himself over to God. In seeking God for guidance and his deliverance, Parker recalled:

> During this time, I totally surrendered my life to the Lord Jesus Christ.
>
> I told the Devil that I was putting on my combat boots and preparing for battle, that I was going to stand firm on the word of God. I told him that I did not care if I never slept another wink in my life, I was not going to take another sleeping pill.
>
> That night was terrible. I never slept a second.
>
> But after that, God did deliver me from that sleeping problem. It went away because I was in His will.
>
> The Lord then impressed upon me to tell my two associates that we were not going to go into business together as planned, that He was leading me in another direction. I

literally cried out God. I told Him I needed the men but that I would make a covenant with Him and that I would do my best with His help.

I then went to my two associates and told them we would have to organize separate businesses. I showed them a list of eight customers and told them to pick four. I took the rest.

These men went their way, and I went my way. The two were very upset with me at first, because they did not understand that I was doing God's will.[18]

According to Parker, "I made a covenant. I was up in the mountains and I said, 'God, I'm scared. I don't know what I'm supposed to do, but I'll try because I think this is what [Y]ou want.'"[19]

As Parker later reflected, it is his relationship with Jesus that keeps him focused. As to the purpose behind "Covenant" in the company name, he continued,"...[I]t shows my relationship with the Lord. This Covenant is a lot bigger than David Parker. Without [H]is assistance, I couldn't run this. During the bad times, if I didn't have [H]im to get down on my knees and say, 'What's happening here?' I couldn't do it."[20]

Also, as Covenant Transport drowned in a sea of debt in 1989 and 1990, Parker recalled that he read again and again a verse from the Book of Isaiah that his sister had shown him in the autumn of 1988. This verse, as Parker remembered, said, basically, that "When you go through the river, you will not drown, and when you go through the fire, you will not be burned."[21] Turning to Scripture, he took comfort in this verse.

Parker's Preacher-Leadership Style and Its Impact on Covenant Transport's Employees and Customers

In addition to making a monetary profit, the implementation of religious faith and values in a business context serves as one of the major goals of corporations led by many evangelical Christians. Parker, pursuing a preacher-leader style, made his religious beliefs part of the company's culture. He actively demonstrates his intense, personal prayerfulness and witnessing, noting that although he does not push his religion, "[I]f I have an employee with a sick baby, [I] bring them into my office and we'll pray."[22] This approach may, however, lead to introduce a troubled employee to Jesus.

Parker's preacher-leader style and, in turn, Covenant Transport's religious orientation manifests itself in a number of ways.[23] Voluntary small group prayer meetings, the majority of which are Christian, and Bible studies take place at its corporate headquarters. It now has three ordained ministers on its payroll who work in the Driver Relations Department, performing a variety of roles, including serving in a ministerial capacity as needed.[24] The company employs a family advocate, who assists drivers and their families (and friends) and, on occasion, in-house employees, as well as several driver representatives. Family and friends of drivers can call in and speak with the family advocate during business hours or leave messages during off hours to be sent to drivers in their trucks. Covenant Values, a companywide program, strives to keep in the forefront of all its employees the integrity and ideals on which the firm was founded.[25]

Cognizant of the current diversity of its workforce, the firm now provides a private place at its corporate headquarters for people of all faiths to pray upon request.[26] Furthermore, despite its founding and continued existence as a religiously oriented corporation, Covenant Transport maintains it treats all its workers alike. Joey B. Hogan, Covenant's senior vice president and chief financial officer, stated, "We think religion rounds out a person's life, but it is not a prerequisite for hiring or advancement inside the company.[27] One top executive, Ronald B. Pope, the firm's senior vice president for sales and marketing, believes in God, but does not adhere to any organized religion, yet he advanced within the organization. However, he asserted, "If you lack character, morality, ethics and the desire to work hard, you won't go forward in the company.'[28]

Drivers form the heart of Covenant's business. During boom times, the firm candidly noted, "Competition for drivers is intense in the trucking industry. There historically has been, and continues to be, an industry-wide shortage of qualified drivers."[29] However, as a result of the number of bankrupt trucking companies in 2001-2002, by early 2003, the company experienced no difficulties in attracting an adequate supply of qualified drivers.[30]

Although employee (and former employee) critics of the company exist,[31] many of the firm's drivers are drawn by its religious principles despite the long hours truckers face and relatively low pay. As one of the firm's drivers stated, "I don't profess their religion, or go to their church. But their reputation is that it's an honest company and I found it to be absolutely true."[32] At its voluntary, fifteen-minute prayer meetings, held each Wednesday at its main terminal in Chattanooga, at which any employee may attend if they wishes, drivers may call in beforehand and request a prayer; if he or she are on the road they can pullover during the scheduled prayer time.[33] Drivers can also take along with them Covenant's free scriptural pamphlets and audio cassettes.[34]

The company holds weekly orientation sessions for its new drivers on Mondays and Wednesdays. There, David Parker, via video, speaks to emphasize the value that the firm places on each individual driver. The orientation primarily serves to familiarize new and returning drivers with company policies and the basic principles of being a good, over-the-road driver. The manager of Employee Support, a minister, opens each session with brief prayer and words of encouragement.[35]

One of Covenant's ministers, Rev. Eugene Coleman, recalled that at the orientations he thanked God for sending the new drivers to the firm and asked that God give them a long, prosperous career there. Reflecting a key evangelical tenet, Coleman emphasized that God was the real director of the company.[36]

In the trucking business, driver turnover constitutes one of the costliest factors affecting a firm's profitability. The cost of turnover is high averaging $6,500 to $8,500 to recruit, screen and train a new driver.[37] Despite its efforts, including a competitive pay scale and striving to get drivers home when they need to, Covenant's driver turnover is somewhat higher than the industry's average of roughly 100 percent a year.[38] However, long-haul drivers have a higher turnover figure of about 130 per year than drivers generally in the trucking sector.[39]

Furthermore, other factors impact on driver turnover, notably compensation. For example, in the third quarter of 1998, Parker estimated that the three cents per mile driver pay raise reduced the firm's annualized driver turnover by about 15 percent. A further increase in driver pay in the fourth quarter by 2.5 cents per mile helped reduce driver turnover by another 10 percent.[40]

The firm's customers see its religious orientation. It hauls cigarettes, but not alcohol or pornography. Biblical scrolls appear on its truck trailers as does Parker's anti-abortion message: "It's not a choice. It is a child."[41] Although candidly admitting that some object to this message, according to Parker, most support it. However, the firm has lost some customers because of this statement.[42]

Environmental Matters: A Minor Blemish

In 1995, during the construction of its new headquarters, both the City of Chattanooga and the State of Tennessee cited the firm for violating storm water regulations and for altering a stream without permits in violation of state statutes and regulations. Even after receiving a notice of violation, the firm cleared and dug another fifty acres after disturbing twenty-five acres, altering one half mile of stream beds and more than two acres of protected wetlands. Although the company maintained its contractors clearing the property had obtained the appropriate permits, Tennessee water pollution control regulators ordered Covenant to restore and enhance the stream, two acres of wetlands, and ninety acres it denuded of vegetation as well as imposing a fine of nearly $59,000. Furthermore, the state did not issue Covenant Transport a stream-alteration permit. State environmental officials, however, authorized the firm's implementation of a plan allowing it to replace wetlands previously impacted in clearing the land.[43]

* * *

The study of how Parker built a publicly held company from virtually nothing, except his knowledge of and experience in the industry, may help others, particularly entrepreneurs, have a better chance of becoming successful in any endeavor of their choosing. Noteworthy is Parker's focus on customer service and his use of cutting-edge technology. Covenant Transport, like Interstate Batteries, represents a company that presents its religion on it sleeve. However, not all firms led by evangelicals pursue this approach.

Notes

1. David R. Parker, "Sermon Story: The Covenant," *Chattanooga Free Press*, May 13, 1995, B1.
2. Covenant Transport, Inc., Prospectus (October 28, 1994), 4.
3. Ibid., 19; Parker "Sermon Story"; email to author from Rick Towe, Vice President, Covenant Transport, Inc., January 27, 2003; Davis, "Transportation Pack: Trucking a Calling for Convenant," *Chattanooga Times*, February 20, 1995, A8; Lance Coleman, "Trucking Execs Say Succeed By Hiring People Better Than Them," *Chattanooga Times/Chattanooga Free Press*, May 16, 1999, Business Section, H5.
4. Covenant Transport, Prospectus, 19.
5. Ibid., 9.

6.   David R. Parker and Jacqueline F. Parker, U.S. Securities and Exchange Commission (SEC) Form 13 G/A (February 11, 2003), 1. The sale of one million shares in a secondary offering will reduce the Parkers' owenership to 38.4 percent. Covenant Transport, Inc. Amendment No. 1 to SEC Form S-3, filed October 31, 2003, 19.
7.   Covenant Transport, Inc., SEC Form 10-K For the Fiscal Year Ended December 31, 2002 (March 28, 2003), 4, 12, 14-17.
8.   David Cullen, "End of the Road?," *Fleet Owner* 96:6 (June 2001): 26-30, provides background on driver teams.
9.   Covenant Transport, SEC Form 10-K, 4; Bear, Stearns & Co., Inc. "Covenant Transport, Inc." (January 30, 2003), n.p.
10. Covenant Transport, SEC Form 10-K, 2-4, 12; A.G. Edwards, "Covenant Transport," (January 31, 2003), 1, 13-14.
11. Covenant Transport, SEC Form 10-K, 2; Bear Stearns Global Transportation & Logistics Special, *Wall Street Transcript*, "Interview with David R. Parker" (May 2002), n.p.
12. Ibid.
13. Covenant Transport, SEC Form 10-K, 3; Covenant Transport, Prospectus, 4, 21.
14. Daniel Machalaba, "More Employees Are Seeking Worship God on the Job," *Wall Street Journal*, June 25, 2002, B1, B12.
15. Ibid.; Randall Balmer, *Encyclopedia of Evangelicalism* (Louisville, KY: Westminister John Knox, 2002), 242, 446.
16. Parker, "Sermon Story."
17. Ibid.
18. Ibid.
19. Davis, "Transportation Pact."
20. Coleman, "Trucking Execs"; Towe email.
21. Parker, "Sermon Story." Isaiah 43:2 states: "When you pass through the waters, I will be with you; and when you pass through the rivers, they will not sweep over you. When you walk through the fire, you will not be burned; the flames will not set you ablaze."
22. Machalaba, "More Employees," B12.
23. Ibid.
24. For background on workplace chaplains, see Rachel Emma Silverman, "More Chaplains Take Ministering Into Workplace," *Wall Street Journal*, November 27, 2001, B1 and Chris L. Jenkins, "Pastors Find Their Work With Workers," *Washington Post*, September 10, 2000, A1.
25. Towe email.
26. Ibid.
27. Machalaba, "More Employees," B12.
28. Ibid.
29. Covenant Transport, SEC Form 10-K, 24.
30. A.G. Edwards, "Covenant Transport," 11; Transcript, Conference Call, Q4 2002 Covenant Transport Earnings, January 29, 2003, n.p. (statement of David R. Parker).
31. See RealDrivers.com, Covenant Transport, BAD Company Reports by Truck Drivers for Truck Drivers!, available at http:// badlist.imess.net/covenant.htm.
32. Machalaba, "More Employees," B12.
33. Towe email; Pam Belluck, "Drivers Find New Service at Truck Stop: Old-Time Religion," *New York Times*, February 1, 1998, A1.
34. Machalaba, "More Employees," B12.
35. Towe email; Covenant Transport, Prospectus, 22.
36. Eugene Coleman, "Sermon Story: The Covenant Opry," *Chattanooga Free Press*, January 3, 1998, C1.

37. Julie Rodriguez et al., *The Cost of Truckload Driver Turnover* (Fargo, ND: Upper Great Plains Transportation Institute, n.d.), ii, 8-9, 11 (mail study conducted in October 1998).

38. Machalaba, "More Employees," B12; *Trucking Economic Review*, "Soft Landing," 2:3 (Third Quarter, 2000): 1-4, at 4.

39. Towe email.

40. Covenant Transport, Inc., Press Release, "Covenant Transport Announces Record Third Quarter Revenue and Earnings," October 14, 1998; Covenant Transport, Inc., Press Release, "Covenant Transport Announces Record Fourth Quarter and Annual Revenue and Earnings," January 27, 1999.

41. Machalaba, "More Employees," B12.

42. Ibid.

43. *In the Matter of Covenant Transport, Inc.*, State of Tennessee, Department of Environment and Conservation, Division of Water Pollution Control, Case No. 95-0476, Order and Assessment, September 28, 1995. John Lane, "Covenant Transport Project For New Headquarters Rolls On," *Chattanooga Times*, December 26, 1995, B4; *Chattanooga Free Press*, "One Trucking Project Rolls," November 12, 1995, H1; *Chattanooga Free Press*, "Trucking Firm Slapped By Environmental Fines," October 10, 1995, B1; Pam Sohn, "State Frowns on Covenant Company," *Chattanooga Times*, October 10, 1995, B1; Commercial Appeal (Memphis), "Deity Invoked Amid Environmental Clash," September 14, 1995, 12A; Pam Sohn and Denise Neil, "Prayer, Debate Greet Land-Fix Plan," *Chattanooga Times*, September 13, 1995, B1; Pam Sohn, "Truck Firm Cited," *Chattanooga Times*, May 18, 1995, B1.

4

R.B. Pamplin Corp.: A Religious-Based Corporation Led by Steward-Leaders

The R.B. Pamplin Corp., like Covenant Transport, exemplifies a company led by evangelicals that has consistently demonstrated a religious-orientation. Two Pamplins, father and son, as heads of the privately held Pamplin Corp. illustrate a steward leadership style. Charitable giving, based on the biblical principle of tithing, serves as the keynote of this firm's enduring Christian orientation, providing an inspiration for other top executives and their corporations. However, difficulties at many of its units cloud the future of the Pamplin Corp.

Business Background

Oregon businessman, Robert B. Pamplin, Jr., the holder of eight academic degrees, including doctorates in theology and business, derives his fortune, in part, from the R.B. Pamplin Corp., a conglomerate, founded by his father, Robert B. Pamplin, Sr.[1] The senior Pamplin had spent his entire career with the same company. He joined the Georgia Hardwood Lumber Co. in 1934, then a small lumber wholesaler, eventually becoming chief operating officer in 1955 and then chairman and chief executive officer from 1957 to 1976 of its successor firm, Georgia-Pacific Corp., a publicly held forest products company. Under his nearly two decades of leadership, Georgia-Pacific stock increased in value by a greater percentage then any other public corporation during this period.[2]

Pamplin senior moved his family to Portland, Oregon, after Georgia-Pacific, which became the world's largest plywood and gypsum producer, shifted its headquarters there in 1954. He became a revered business leader in Portland, in large measure because of his charitable endeavors, and secured the family fortune.[3]

When Pamplin, Jr. was eleven and bedridden with hepatitis, weak and jaundiced, the senior Pamplin began reading to him corporate annual reports (first the report to shareholders and then a review of the balance sheet), corporate pamphlets, and, then *Wall Street Journal* articles, thereby passing on the gift of business understanding from father to son. By the time junior had entered high school, dad had taught him about stocks and bonds and how to evaluate a company.[4]

Pamplin, Jr.'s grandmother died when he was in college, leaving him securities worth some $160,000. Borrowing against these holdings, he invested in the stock market, becoming a millionaire at age twenty-two.[5] He continued to make money on his own through other investments, from timberland in the Southeast, to farmland in Oregon, to horse breeding.[6]

In 1957, Pamplin, Sr. organized the R.B. Pamplin Corp. On his mandatory retirement from Georgia-Pacific in 1976, he and junior got R.B. Pamplin Corp. off the ground. Soon thereafter, the Pamplin firm bought Ross Island Sand & Gravel Co. Through acquisitions and internal growth, the conglomerate recorded annual sales approaching an estimated 900 million dollars in 2000, making it the three hundred sixteenth largest firm on the 2001 *Forbes* list of the nation's top 500 privately held corporations.[7]

About 90 percent of Pamplin's sales come from textiles produced by Mount Vernon Mills, Inc. and its subsidiary, Riegel Textile Corp., which together comprise one of the U.S.'s leading producers of denim, textiles for home furnishings, yarn, uniforms and work clothes. While at Georgia-Pacific, Pamplin, Sr., through the Pamplin Corp., began buying shares of Mount Vernon Mills, then a public corporation.[8] By 1982, the Pamplin Corp.'s 10 percent stake (as of 1976) had increased so that it owned about one third of the common stock of Mount Vernon Mills. Then, in 1982 it purchased the remainder.[9] In turn, Mount Vernon Mills acquired Riegel in 1985. Over the years, by investing capital into its plants, Mount Vernon Mills has maintained a strong presence in the textile industry, while many other domestic manufacturers were closing plants and even filing for bankruptcy.

The Pamplin Corp.'s current corporate umbrella also includes two major units: first, construction materials, concrete and asphalt, including Ross Island Sand & Gravel Co. and second, Pamplin Communications Corp. This latter entity serves as the parent corporation for a variety of entities including the Pamplin Broadcasting Corp., which operates radio stations broadcasting local news and talk shows throughout Oregon and Washington State, Christian Supply Centers, Inc., a chain of retail stores in Oregon, Washington, and Idaho offering an array of Christian products, the Oregon Publication Corp., the owner of the *Portland Tribune*, and the Pamplin Music and Entertainment Corp., a producer of *Bible Man* videos and a live, traveling Christian show.[10]

The Pamplins' Religious Orientation

Both Pamplins, senior and junior, received a strong faith in God while growing up. Pamplin, Sr., raised a Methodist, came to believe the Bible as the infallible Word of God. Throughout his life he has focused on salvation for individuals through Jesus and on Christian living on a personal basis.[11]

Daily Bible study supported him both in his personal relationships and his business endeavors. He believed that his success in the business world, first as a manager and executive at Georgia-Pacific and then at the Pamplin Corp. stemmed as much from reading the Bible as from his accounting and financial acumen. Senior and his wife regularly went to sleep, lying in bed reading scriptural passages to each other.[12]

Senior's leadership skills showed he benefits of his strong religious faith. He was filled with a quiet sense of inner peace. His lifetime study of the Bible, made it easier for him to trust his judgment and sense the correctness of his decisions and actions. Facing difficult business decisions, particularly those marked by competing goals, reflecting on Scripture help him think creatively, innovatively. Often, an idea did not come out of the blue. As Pamplin, Jr. recalled, a thought, for his father, "was always moved by God's hand."[13]

Pamplin, Jr., was reared in the First Presbyterian Church in Augusta, Georgia. At an early age, he was exposed to Bible studies at the church, first in Sunday school, where his mother taught, and then in Sunday morning and evening church services. Also, each morning the family gathered at the breakfast table for a devotional, led by his mother who assumed the responsibility for creating a Christian environment at home. As he later reflected, "I must place squarely on my mother's shoulders a generous portion of credit for sealing me as one of Christ's own."[14]

At age eight, Pamplin, Jr., accepted Jesus into his life. The renowned evangelist, Rev. Billy Graham, who would become one of the most recognized religious figures worldwide in the second half of the twentieth century (and who claims to have preached to more people than anyone else in history[15]) was the guest speaker at the Pamplin's church in Augusta. Junior has noted that his most memorable childhood experience was hearing Rev. Graham, then in his early thirties, at the family church. He remembered Graham's "zeal and enthusiasm for Christ were like nothing I had ever encountered."[16] "To be saved," Graham proclaimed that day, "you must accept Jesus Christ into your life, must invite the Holy Spirit of God to live inside you." "Those of you who have made a decision to commit your lives to Christ," Graham called out, "stand up, leave your seats, and walk down the aisle to join me in prayer. You come!"[17] Junior caught Senior's eye as he stood up, seeking approval. His father nodded "Yes." He then went to the church's altar, accepting Jesus into his life and praying with Rev. Graham.

In 1973, Pamplin, Jr. faced a "precipitating crisis." He discovered a mole on his leg. His five-year battle against malignant melanoma, a potentially fatal form of skin cancer, requiring surgery and continued follow-up, led him to reexamine his already deeply held religious beliefs.[18] He recalled, "I realized that even though my business career had been successful, my life lacked greater meaning, and I needed to come up with new notions about what success really meant. I turned closer to God. I had always followed Christian principles, but the brush with death made me want to know more fully and exactly what my faith was all about."[19] As his pain and fear brought him back again to faith, he began taking courses at Portland's Western Conservative Baptist Seminary, ultimately becoming an ordained minister.[20] He came to reaffirm his belief that "our Savior is working through us towards the salvation of all."[21]

A hallmark of Pamplin, Jr.'s faith is his enthusiastic belief that everything in life happens for the best.[22] He based his source for his secure belief on the Apostle Paul's Letter to the Romans: "And we know that in all things God works for the good of those who love [H]im, who have been called according to [H]is purpose" (Romans 8:28).

In 1982, Pamplin, Jr. founded the Christ Community Church in Newberg, Oregon, south of Portland. There he continues to serve as senior pastor and occasionally preaches. By providing food from farms Pamplin, Jr. owns and other sources to various social service agencies in Portland, the church helps to feed the hundreds of indigent people every day.[23] He noted, "All we ask in return is that the agencies provide counseling to help their clients become independent, productive members of society."[24]

Financially, Pamplin, Jr. prospered both on his own and through the Pamplin Corp. with his father. In reflecting on his material success, he stated, "It's not luck, and although I'm not stupid, I know I've had a lot of divine help through this." He attributed his success to not worrying about financial gains, but to making certain he tried to be a caring person who helped those around him. He continued, "I firmly believe that if I changed tomorrow and made the accumulation of wealth my goal, (it would) all come undone and the chain would be broken."[25]

"There are two alternatives," emphasized the younger Pamplin. "One is based on the bottom line." Another, he said, is epitomized by spiritual figures, such as Mahatma Gandhi, Mother Teresa, Albert Schweitzer, and Jesus Christ, and "I defy anyone to tell me they're not more successful than the Donald Trumps of the world."[26]

Over the last three decades, the younger Pamplin repeatedly has pondered: why was he spared? For what purpose? He has offered three explanations. First, "[God] knows the reason, and He loves me. That is enough."[27] Second, "It is clear that God has loved me enough to apply shock treatment to my soul. His direction for my life has come in jolts, always forcing me out of naked dependence on self and back into a humble trust in Him."[28] Third, "And I believe that God spared me so that I might do good for His Kingdom," Pamplin stated. "He had a use for me."[29] Serving God's purpose became manifest in the Pamplins' charitable practices.

Stewardship as Exemplified Through the Pamplins' Charitable Giving

The religious faith of Pamplin, Jr.'s ancestors represented a working faith. In reviewing a thousand years of Pamplin family history, he wrote, "My forebears didn't closet their belief away in ritual and mystery. They acted out God's laws day by day. In their every least dealing they demonstrated that the human mind is a gift from God, and thus to be used for His greater glory, rather than for rationalizing some way around His canon."[30]

Early in their marriage, Pamplin, Sr. and his wife followed the biblical principle of tithing (Genesis 14:20 and 28:22; Deuteronomy

14:22). Tithing involves setting aside at least 10 percent of one's pretax income for philanthropic endeavors. Pamplin, Sr. believed that part of what God had put in his hands should be given back gratefully. By sharing his money with others he removed its power over him, thereby restoring the preeminence of God from "Whom All Blessings Flow."[31]

Initially, they gave 10 percent of what Pamplin, Sr. made to charity. As a middle-aged couple, they raised their charitable contributions to 30 percent of his pretax income.[32] As he reflected, "It has been the hand of God on this company [Georgia-Pacific] that made it grow so fast. He has seen to it that I've received benefits far in excess of what I've given. For me not to give still more in return would be like stealing from the Lord."[33] The more money they gave away, the more the Pamplins seemed to have.

Pamplin, Sr. and his wife, a deeply religious couple, taught their son, Pamplin, Jr., an only child, that he had an obligation not only to better himself but also to help those less fortunate around him. This philosophy served to guide the younger Pamplin throughout his life. His wealth entered into the equation, enabling him to do much.

Pamplin, Jr., calls his philosophy the "Next Generation," believing it is his duty to pass on his good fortune.[34] He tries to integrate his charitable work into nearly every aspect of the Pamplin firm, now serving as its president and chief executive officer. For Pamplin and many other evangelical executives, capitalism makes a virtue of charity by creating wealth for giving. Philanthropic donations, both personally and by their corporations, exemplify their stewardship and accountability to God and Jesus. As Pamplin Jr. recalled, "[At Western Seminary] I learned why I should give—because Christ wants me to. Before, I had participated in a lot of fund-raising campaigns, but I did it because it was just another activity I could chalk up on my resume."[35] Looking to a New Testament verse, "Remember this: Whoever sows sparingly will also reap sparingly, and who sows generously will also reap generously" (Corinthians 9:6), he believed, "We always have great faith that if we do the right thing, we will always harvest a great crop. We've not only gained wealth but gained spiritually ourselves and cast some light in which others may walk."[36]

The Internal Revenue Code allows corporations to deduct charitable contributions up to 10 percent of their annual taxable income.[37]

However, average corporate charitable contributions equal slightly more than one percent of domestic pretax income.[38]

R.B. Pamplin Corp., through its major subsidiary Mount Vernon Mills, has regularly contributed 10 percent of its pretax income to charitable organizations.[39] In 2000, for example, on operating (pretax) profits of $108 million,[40] the Pamplin Corp.'s contributions amounted to over $10 million. These contributions went to nearly two hundred charities nationwide.[41]

At Mount Vernon Mills, where employees at each of its plants decide where philanthropic dollars go, particular attention is focused on community-related giving, including a $2 million contribution to build a new school in Trion, Georgia, the location of one of its key plants.[42] The firm also sponsors scholarship programs in each of the communities where its plants are located, providing about one hundred fifty scholarships annually.[43]

The Relationship of the Pamplin Corporation to Its Stakeholders: Another Example of Stewardship

In addition to charitable giving, the Pamplins, Sr. and Jr., live their religious faith and a belief in stewardship as a value through the Pamplin Corp's relationships with its various stakeholders: shareholders, employees, and the community. They demonstrated their sense of responsibility not only through charitable donations but also in the operations of the firm's core subsidiary, Mount Vernon Mills.

Pamplin, Jr.'s approach goes back to the senior Pamplin, who saw corporate success as a three-legged stool, balancing the interests of shareholders, employees, and the communities where its employees live and work. Pamplin, Sr. regarded the interests of these three elements as equal. Shareholders are entitled to a "fair" return on their money. To build earnings for shareholders, he financed corporate expansion through debt, not equity, and invested in new, modernized plants. Regarding employees as essential, he made certain they received competitive wages and benefits as well as incentives to perform at their peak. He also took an active interest in the communities where Georgia-Pacific operated, encouraging volunteer efforts by employees in these communities. He made certain the company was a good corporate citizen, especially with respect to charitable donations for education.[44]

This approach, which Pamplin, Sr. developed at Georgia-Pacific, became the guiding business philosophy for the Pamplin Corp.'s operation of Mount Vernon Mills. Specifically, Mount Vernon Mills regards the interests of its three stakeholders, namely, its shareholders (in this case, the Pamplin Corp.), its employees, and the communities where each of its plant is located, as equal. Mount Vernon Mills proclaims: "Because of this, no one interest is any more important than any other in the total company equation. It is therefore incumbent upon all to work together in harmony, because each is so closely tied."[45]

Its Trion, Georgia plant, the world's largest denim facility, represents the centerpiece of the efforts of Mount Vernon Mills to focus on people, manufacturing, and spending.[46] At Trion, employees weave denim fabric and finish it for sale to major manufacturers of jeans for men, women, and children. The Trion plant had its roots in the Trion Co. formed before the Civil War. In 1912, B. D. Riegel bought the mill, which subsequently became part of the Riegel Textile Corp. in the 1940s. In 1985, Trion became part of the Pamplin textile business when Mount Vernon Mills acquired Riegel. Trion was (and remains) a company town. Nearly everyone who lives in Trion has a connection to the mill.

State of the art equipment and technology, resulting in higher productivity and products nearly free from defects, enable the Trion facility to keep a leg up on the competition, foreign and domestic, and to prosper despite ever-increasing textile imports. Over the years, Mount Vernon Mills invested heavily in the plants it has kept open. Since Riegel became part of Mount Vernon Mills in 1985, the firm poured over $270 million into the Trion plant alone.[47]

In addition to heavy capital spending, mainly on new equipment, Mount Vernon Mills' success at Trion rests on its commitment to its customers, including the timely delivery of high quality goods, and an emphasis on a family atmosphere among its employees.[48] At Trion, the Pamplin subsidiary strives to fulfill its mission to be the supplier of choice for its customers through superior order fulfillment, among other customer service attributes. Its "passion for perfection"[49] has led to a consistency of product quality.

Employees represent a key asset for the Pamplins. As Pamlin, Jr., stated, "Taking care of our employees is very important; loving our neighbor as ourselves is the second commandment. If one sows bountifully to humankind, he will reap bountifully."[50]

At Trion, the firm offers extensive employee training. For all of its employees (at Trion and elsewhere), Mount Vernon Mills is a textile industry leader in funding employee retirement benefits.[51]

As evangelists who live their commitment through stewardship, evidenced by charitable giving and building sound relationships, the Pamplins impact on their employees in a positive manner. For instance, many of Mount Vernon's employees are "committed Christians like the two men [Senior and Junior Pamplin] at the top. They appreciate working for a father and son who've set good examples of being equally committed to success in business and to good works as Christians."[52]

The Environment: Pamplin's Shadow

Despite these positive attainments and a longstanding Pamplin family traits of moral rectitude and social responsibility,[53] the Pamplin Corp. encountered environmental dilemmas both at the Mount Vernon Mills' Trion plant and the operations of the Ross Island Sand & Gravel Co.

With the expansion of Mount Vernon Mills' denim plant at Trion, the plant annually released millions of gallons of textile waste into the town's water waste and sewage treatment facility, although the facility was unequipped to handle it. Dyes (more technically, suspended solids) from the plant on the Chattanooga River would get into the river, giving the river's sides and bottom a stark blue or black color. Gradually over several years, realizing that the plant's waste outran the municipal facility's ability to handle it, Mount Vernon Mills and the town began to work together to come up with a solution to the problem. A citizen's lawsuit brought in 1993 against the town under the federal Clean Water Act by the Georgia Environmental Organization accelerated the negotiations between the town and Mount Vernon Mills, forcing the firm to spend millions of dollars to halt the pollution. As part of a 1994 settlement, Mount Vernon Mills agreed to upgrade the local waste water and sewage treatment plant, footing about 97 percent of the bill, resulting in the payment of more than $9 million.[54]

The environmental practices of another Pamplin Corp. subsidiary, Ross Island Sand & Gravel Co., have come under scrutiny. In 1999, the Columbia River Gorge Commission fined the Ross Island firm, a landowner, and a lessee $5,000 for excavating exploratory test pits on a parcel of land near Lyle, Washington, without the appropriate permits.[55]

Also in 1999, the Oregon Department of Environmental Quality ruled that the Pamplin subsidiary violated the state's landfill laws by illegally dumping solid waste (timber, wood and metal debris) from 1985 to 1999 at Ross Island, located just upstream on the Willamette River from downtown Portland. By failing to have a permit to operate a solid waste disposal site, regulators asserted that the firm created an unauthorized landfill on the island. In a settlement, the company paid a fine of some $6,300 and agreed to an environmental remediation program.[56]

The Ross Island subsidiary now faces a potentially massive liability from the cost of reclaiming the island which it began excavating in 1926 (but ceased mining operations there in 2001).[57] In 2000, state authorities discovered (as subsequently acknowledged by corporate executives) that the firm repeatedly filed erroneous annual reports with the City of Portland, greatly underestimating the annual amount of material mined from the island since 1981. The Oregon Division of State Lands required the Ross Island firm to return the 300-acre site to as close to its natural condition as possible. According to some estimates, reclamation might have involved obtaining upwards of twenty to thirty-five million cubic yards of sand and filling Ross Island's lagoon, a resting spot for migrating salmon as well as a bird feeding and nesting area, which was excavated to a depth of 130 feet. The Ross Island firm responded by proposing to add 4.5 million cubic yards of clean fill, at an estimated cost of $3 million, over a period of ten years, to help restore the heavily mined Willamette River island to a more natural condition. State regulators accepted the company's scaled-down reclamation plan, recognizing that filling more of the lagoon would be impractical. Pamplin, Jr. also promised to give the island to the City of Portland by the end of 2004 and provide an endowment for the island's maintenance and monitoring, with the company continuing to meet the reclamation plan.[58]

A Look Ahead

Besides these environment difficulties and its generally reactive approach, the Pamplin Corp. faces other challenges in the early years of the twenty-first century. In November 2001, the firm closed its Nashville-based, Pamplin Music subsidiary, a producer and distributor of contemporary Christian CDs and albums, after six money-losing years. Its high profile, print media venture, the *Portland Tribune*, may be in jeopardy, after sustaining loses of between $8 and $10 million annually.[59] Most importantly, its textile operations face increasing pressure from low-cost foreign competitors, resulting in plant closings and employee layoffs.[60] At some point, lower overseas wage rates and low-cost imports, coupled with the likely lifting of U.S. quotas on apparel and textile imports, offset investments in modern equipment technology as well as the company's focus on providing superior customer service.

Viewing these challenges as opportunities, not problems, Pamplin, Jr. declared, "[S]o my greater family's most durable element has been its skill at solving, facilitating, and overcoming differences." He continued:

> Yet I must emphasize that it's an angel who brings us these solvents, this ability to compromise and fix. The true toolmaker, I believe unalterably, is Christ our Savior. My forebearers didn't surmount the hardships they faced simply in order to make a handful of recent Pamplins rich. They experienced God's justice, rather, because they kept in mind the greater betterment of all God's family. Given a firm allegiance to the Divine, and an unyielding awareness that Christian meaning pervades every action, they couldn't help but prevail.[61]

Only time will tell whether the younger Pamplin can devise innovative solutions to the challenges the Pamplin Corp. faces and (it will encounter) that will work to the benefit of everyone involved.

Notes

1. Dr. Robert B. Pamplin, Jr. et al., *Heritage* (New York: Mastermedia 1994), 324.
2. Dr. Norman Vincent Peale, "Foreword" to *Heritage*, xi. Dr. Peale, a renowned twentieth-century minister and best selling author, emphasized prayer and the centrality of Jesus as a source of power for Christians. Randall Balmer, *Encyclopedia of Evangelism* (Louisville, KY: Westminster John Knox, 2002), 442.
3. Pamplin, *Heritage*, 321-322; Carleen Hawn, "Don't Call Me Eccentric," *Forbes* 164:11 (November 1, 1999): 124-126, at 126.
4. Pamplin, *Heritage*, 292-293, 377-378, 412; Robert B. Pamplin, Jr. "Manager's Journal: Fathers and Sons Working Together," *Wall Street Journal*, June 20, 1994, A12.
5. Pamplin, *Heritage*, 342-343, 475; Jeff Favre, "Like Father; A Businessman Searches His Heritage for Character Patterns," Chicago Tribune, November 6, 1994, Tempo Section, 4; William DiBenedetto, "Portland Businessmen Traces Family History Back to Crusades," *Journal of Commerce*, October 17, 1994, 14A.
6. Pamplin, *Heritage*, 412-416, 441-445.
7. *Forbes*, "500 Largest Private Corporations," 168:13 (November 26, 2001): 162-198, at 182. The firm was ranked 266 in 1999 and 300 in 2000. *Forbes*, "500

56   Evangelical Christian Executives

Biggest Private Companies," 164:14 (December 13, 1999): 167-240, at 218; *Forbes*, "The Top 500 Private Companies," 166:14 (November 27, 2000): 179-240, at 212.
8.   *Pamplin, Heritage*, 344.
9.   Ibid., 345-346, 356-357.
10. R.B. Pamplin Corporation, available at http://www.pamplin. org; Andy Dworkin, "An Old-Economy Evangelist," *The Oregonian*, April 2, 2000, B1.
11. Pamplin, *Heritage*, 340.
12. Ibid., 259, 279.
13. Ibid., 318.
14. Ibid., 378. See also Ibid., 291, 293.
15. Balmer, *Encyclopedia*, 252; Robert H. Krapol and Charles H. Lippy, *The Evangelicals: A Historical, Thematic, and Bibliographical Guide* (Westport, CT: Greenwood, 1999), 247. Mark A. Noll discusses the significance of Rev. Graham in *American Evangelical Christianity: An Introduction* (Malden, MA: Blackwell, 2001), 44-55.
16. *Pamplin, Heritage*, 379.
17. Ibid., 291.
18. Ibid., Heritage, 425, 427-433.
19. "Question & Answer: Do You Have Fun Giving?," Interview with Robert B. Pamplin, *Reformed Quarterly* 20:1 (Spring 2001): 10-11, at 11.
20. *Pamplin*, Heritage, 434-435.
21. Ibid., 477.
22. Ibid., 384, 435, 453.
23. Ibid., 509-510; "Do You Have Fun Giving," at 11; Siobhan Lougram, "Breakfast with Bob," *Oregonian*, January 19, 1999, Fooday Section, FD1.
24. *Pamplin, Heritage*, 510.
25. *Favre*, "Like Father."
26. Joseph L. McCarthy, "Through the Needle's Eye: The Spiritual CEO," *Chief Executive (U.S.)* 110 (January/February 1996): 49-51, at 50.
27. Pamplin, *Heritage*, 435.
28. Ibid., 434.
29. Ibid.; See also John H. Taylor, "Creative Philanthropy," *Forbes* 150:9, October 19, 1992: 64-66, at 66;
30. Pamplin, *Heritage*, 499.
31. Ibid., 296.
32. Ibid., 279, 297.
33. Ibid., 335.
34. Dan McGraw, "The Christian Capitalists," *U.S. World News & Report* 118:10 (March 1995): 52-62, at 60.
35. "Do You Have Fun Giving?," at 11.
36. Ibid. Beyond the scope of this book, the Pamplin family and Pamplin Foundation fund many educational, human services, historic preservation, and arts programs. Taylor, "Creative Philanthropy," 65-66; Hawn, "Don't Call Me Eccentric."
37. Internal Revenue Code § 170(b)(2).
38. Sophia A. Muirhead, Corporate Contributions in 2001 (New York: The Conference Board, 2003), 8; The Center on Philanthropy at Indiana University, *Giving U.S.A. 2001: The Annual Report on Philanthropy for the Year 2000* (Indianapolis, IN: American Association of Fund-Raising Counsel Trust for Philanthropy, 2001), 77.
39. Pamplin, *Heritage*, 360; John W. McCurry et al., "Mount Vernon: A Passion for Perfection," *Textile World* 148:6 (June 1998): 36-54, at 42, 48.
40. Forbes, "500 Largest Private Companies," at 182.

41. R.B. Pamplin Corp.: Philanthropy, available at http://www. pamplin.org/philan-thropy-content.html
42. Ibid.; Mount Vernon Mills: Passion For Perfection, available at http:// www.mvmills.com/html; McCurry, "Mount Vernon," at 48.
43. Mount Vernon: Passion For Perfection.
44. Pamplin, *Heritage*, 320-321.
45. Mount Vernon Mills: Corporate Citizens, available at http:// www.mvmills.com/html/company/citizens.htm.
46. For background on the Trion plant, I have drawn on Mike Pare, "Mount Vernon Mills Invests to Compete," *Chattanooga Times/ Chattanooga Free Press*, May 21, 2000, Business Section, G1; John Vass, Jr., "Model Trion Mill," *Chattanooga Free Press*, August 16, 1998, Business Section, 8; Randall Higgins, "Mill Lasts Like Denim," *Chattanooga Times*, May 6, 1996, Regional Section, B8.
47. Letter to author from Dr. R.B. Pamplin, Jr., January 23, 2003.
48. McCurry, "Mount Vernon," at 38, 42, 44, 47.
49. Ibid., 38. See Jeffrey Pfeffer, *The Human Equation: Building Profits By Putting People First* (Boston: Harvard Business School, 1998), 48, who emphasizes the importance of inventory management as well as quality and delivery performance in the competitive success of domestic apparel manufacturers.
50. "Do You Have Fun Giving?," at 11.
51. McCurry, "Mount Vernon," at 54.
52. Pamplin, *Heritage*, 359.
53. 53.Pamplin, *Heritage*, 499.
54. *Georgia Environmental Organization, Inc. v Town of Trion*, Consent Order, ND 4:93 CV 0365 HLM (ND Ga 1994); Sean Reilly, "Down the Drain: Getting Toxic Waste Out of Public Sewers," *E* 2:9 (March/April 1998): 26-27; Telephone interview by author with E.G. Cochrane, Vice President and General Counsel, Mount Vernon Mills, Inc., January 28, 2003; Email to Matthew Mantel, Reference Librarian, Jacob Burns Law Library, The George Washington University Law School from Albert Palmour, January 6, 2003.
55. *In the Matter of Protection of Scenic, Cultural, Natural, and Recreation Resources in the Columbia River Gorge National Scenic Area From Land Use Violations on a Parcel of Land Owned by Elizabeth Cole*, Consent Decree and Order, Columbia River Gorge Commission, July 13, 1999; Richard Read, "Ross Island Gravel May Move Mining," *The Oregonian*, September 10, 1999, Business Section, 1.
56. Letter from Charles W. Donaldson, Manager, Solid Waste Permits, Northwestern Region, Oregon Department of Environmental Quality to A. Charles Steinwandel, Executive Vice President, Ross Island Sand & Gravel Co., January 22, 1999; Letter from Roger D. Dilts, Environmental Law Specialist, Oregon Department of Environmental Quality, Enforcement Section to Tom Lindley, Perkins Coie, LLP, July 2, 1999; Brent Walth, "Ross Island Owner Dumped Waste Illegally," *Oregonian*, January 27, 1999, Local Section, D1. Also, sediments disposed of by the company on Ross Island between 1986 and 1991 allegedly contained contamination, including oil, grease, and paint chips. Ibid.
57. Scott Learn, "Portland Ross Island Plan Backed," *Oregonian*, August 28, 2002, D3; Scott Learn, "Island Plan Gets Mixed Grades," *Oregonian*, July 17, 2002, C1; Fred Leeson, "Ross Island Company Proposes 'Clean' Fill for Restoration," *The Oregonian*, June 4, 2002, B1; Nigel Jaquiss, "The Incredible Shrinking Empire of Bob Pamplin," *Willamette Weekly*, January 30, 2002, 1; Tomoko Hosaka, "Legislator Tries to Bury Talk of Ross Island Dump Site," *The Oregonian*, February 28, 2001, D1; Steve Duin, "No Island Is a Man, Save Bob Pamplin's," *The Oregonian*,

May 21, 2000, B1; Brent Walth and Scott Learn, "State May Stop Mining of Ross Island," *Oregonian*, April 26, 2000, A1.

58.   Fred Leeson, "State To Accept Plan To Restore Ross Island," Oregonian, June 10, 2003, A1.

59.   Jaquiss, "Incredible Shrinking Empire."

60.   See, e.g., Robert Rodriguez and Dennis Pollock, "Mill to ClosePlant in Fresno," *Fresno Bee*, January 10, 2003, A1.

61.   Pamplin, *Heritage*, 469.

5

The ServiceMaster Co.: From a Religious to a Secular, Spiritual-Orientation

The top executives at ServiceMaster, today a publicly held *Fortune* 500 corporation, built an organization around strong religious faith and clearly defined values. The firm rests the vision and efforts in the pursuit of excellence of four individuals: Marion E. Wade, Kenneth N. Hansen, Sr., Kenneth T. Wessner, and C. William Pollard. It grew from humble origins, led first by a preacher-steward-leader and then by a succession of CEOs, who combined preacher-steward-servant leadership styles. More recently, the organization, now led by a non-evangelical CEO and chairman, follows an inclusive, secular-spiritual stance. Coincidentally with this transition, the firm's legal difficulties mounted. Its post-1998 profits plummeted and then rebounded in 2002 to the levels of 1999 and 2000.

Business Background

The roots of ServiceMaster go back to 1929, when Marion E. Wade, an evangelical Baptist, started a moth-proofing business out of his home in Chicago. As Wade candidly admitted in his autobiography:

If today I applied for an executive position with the company [ServiceMaster] of which I am chairman of the board of Directors, I wouldn't even be granted an interview. My application form would be dismally brief. Before going into my present business I played semiprofessional baseball for a few years. I sold insurance for a few years, and I sold aluminumware for a few more years, none of which would make me of particular value to a thriving corporation. Moreover, I couldn't boast of a college degree, not even a high school diploma, and my record in grammar school wouldn't mark me as the one most likely to succeed. Though I started the company myself, I had no business experience or acumen which might have given me the slightest hope that it would one day become the leader in its field. I didn't even think of that; I was merely trying to earn a living during the worst period of America's economic history. Despite my personal shortcomings and the company's hazardous beginnings, the fact remains that ServiceMaster has thrived.[1]

After World War II, Wade expanded into the carpet cleaning business, again locally based in the Chicago area. Because he was already sending employees into people's homes, Wade could now offer two services, not just mothproofing.

After meeting Robert Wenger, a Roman Catholic, who at the time was a sales representative for one of the nation's largest rug manufacturers, they formed Wade, Wenger & Associates, on January 1, 1947.[2] Providing on-location (in the home) cleaning and maintenance services, the firm flourished. In 1961, the firm changed its name to Wade Wenger ServiceMaster Co., becoming known as ServiceMaster Industries, Inc. in 1967. Wade served as chairman of the board from 1947 to 1973.

Even before joining with Wenger, Wade had met Kenneth N. Hansen, Sr., a Wheaton College graduate, at a church service when Hansen was an interim pastor in the winter of 1942-1943.[3] Wheaton College, in suburban Chicago, is an elite Christian college that numbers the Rev. Billy Graham as one of its graduates.[4] Wade invited Hansen to work for him and ultimately Hansen did so. Hansen served as the firm's chief executive officer from 1957 to 1975 and as chairman of the board from 1973 to 1981. He oversaw the firm's growth from a carpet cleaning company with fewer than ten employees and annual revenues of $125,000 to a multi-faceted entity with revenues of some $500 million by 1981. Hansen focused on phasing-out of company-owned branches for home cleaning services and replacing them with franchises. He helped lead the firm into new service areas, particularly the management of housekeeping in hospitals.[5] Under Hansen, the company went public in 1962.

Then, under the leadership of Kenneth T. Wessner, ServiceMaster actively expanded into commercial maintenance and cleaning for hospitals and schools. Wessner, who began as a ServiceMaster field service manager and then held a variety of supervisory positions in its franchise business, served as the chief executive officer from 1975 to 1983 and chairman of the board from 1981 to 1990.

Wessner started the firm's healthcare business in 1962. Thereafter, the company came to emphasize cleaning, food, laundry, grounds and landscaping, facilities operations and maintenance services, and total facilities management for education and healthcare institutions as well as factories. In 1975, when the he became CEO, the firm had revenues of $143 million; fifteen years later at the end of Wessner's chairmanship, its revenues had exploded to over $2 billion.[6] Nearly all of its growth was internal.

Reflecting his passionate devotion to perfection, in heading ServiceMaster, Wessner emphasized the importance of small details. In pointing out the window between a cafeteria and a kitchen at the firm's headquarters, Wessner noted, "We put that in because we think it's a good idea in food service. A window helps remind everyone about the importance of cleanliness to customers."[7]

C. William Pollard, a former corporate attorney, professor and college administrator at Wheaton College, transformed ServiceMaster, pursuing a growth-oriented approach based on an aggressive acquisition strategy. After joining the company in 1977, he served as the firm's chief executive officer from 1983 to 1993 and again from 1999 to 2001 and as chairman of the board from 1990 to 2002.

For a long period, the firm thrived. From 1973 to 1985, for example, under Wessner and Pollard, ServiceMaster's return on equity was the highest of all large service or industrial companies in the United States, averaging more than thirty percent annually after taxes.[8] Pollard concluded that the firm would have to develop or acquire new lines of business if it were to continue to double in size every five years. It opted for external growth.

Beginning in the mid-1980s, the firm adapted its expertise to new markets to generate the growth requisite for increased profitability. Pollard saw opportunities to provide added services to homeowners. ServiceMaster embarked on an expansion into consumer markets, via a series of acquisitions, trying to buy growth by building on its existing network of carpet cleaning franchises. In 1986, it acquired Terminix, a termite pest control service, for $167 million in cash, followed by Merry Maids, a home cleaning service, for $25 million in cash in 1988. Then, in bought American Home Shield, a provider of home appliance and systems warranty service contracts, for $96 million of its stock in 1989, and two residential lawn care services, TruGreen in 1990 in return for 20 percent interest in ServiceMaster and ChemLawn for $103 million in cash in 1992. It continued its acquisition spree in the late 1990s, purchasing AmeriSpec, a home inspection service, for $7 million of cash in 1996; another residential lawn care service, Barefoot, in 1997 for $237 million ($90 million in cash and $147 million in ServiceMaster stock); Rescue Industries, a drain cleaning and plumbing repair service, for $74 million ($71 million in cash and $3 million in its stock); and Ruppert

Landscape, a commercial landscaping firm for $58 million ($24 million in cash and $34 million in its shares) in 1998. In 1999, it acquired American Residential Services, a firm offering heating and air conditioning, plumbing and electrical repair services for home and commercial buildings, for $292 million in cash, LandCare USA, a commercial landscaping service 1999 for $331 million, consisting of $140 million in cash and $191 million in its shares, and Landscape, another commercial landscaping firm, for $131 million, with $75 million paid in cash and $56 million of its shares.[9]

These acquisitions, particularly those consummated in the late 1990s, marked a departure from the firm's usual fiscal conservatism, helping to saddle the company with over $1.7 billion in long-term debt by the end of 2000.[10] By January 2001, its debt had ballooned to nearly $2 billion.[11]

Concurrently with rising debt levels, the firm's profits dropped. For the first time in nearly three decades, ServiceMaster's profits (as restated in 2002), declined from nearly $180 million in 1998 to $153 million in 1999 and 2000, and receded further to $116 million by 2001 only to rebound to $157 million in 2002.[12] The diminution in profits during the 1999-2001 period occurred as a result of three factors: the less than smooth integration of LandCare and American Residential Services; profit margin declines coupled with revenue growth deceleration at its TruGreen unit; and the continued deterioration in the profitability of its management services unit.[13]

A corporate restructuring was clearly in order and it began under Pollard. In 1999, the firm sold a unit that provided cleaning and maintenance services for paint booths used in the auto industry. The next year saw the sale of the unit specializing in the management of long-term care facilities as well as its TruGreen interior plantcare business.[14]

The need for new senior management and even more restructuring led to a search outside ServiceMaster. In February 2001, Jonathan P. Ward, a Presbyterian, formerly president and chief operating officer of R.R. Donnelley & Sons Co., became its first non-evangelical president and chief executive officer, bringing new energy and a willingness to make difficult decisions, in part, because of his "outsider" status. Ward, trained as an engineer, brought his marketing and operations reputation to his new task. In 2002, Ward, who continued as CEO, became chairman of the board, succeeding Pollard as board chair, who remained a director until 2003, with Ernest J.

Morzek, a long-term ServiceMaster executive, named as president and chief operating officer.

Ward saw as his first priority the need to increase shareholder value, focusing on those units that would provide both the greatest return and have the highest potential for growth. Reflecting a modern managerial orientation, he noted, "We will focus our management talent and financial resources on the consumer businesses, which serve markets where we have leadership positions, higher margins, and greater long-term growth prospects and give us the greatest opportunity to increase shareholder value."[15] To this end, Ward instituted a strategic review for all of ServiceMaster's operations.

Recognizing that the firm lacked sufficient capital to invest in both its commercial management and consumer service sectors at the same time, the firm continued to refocus its operations. It sold its struggling commercial management services division that provided maintenance and support services for health care, educational, institutional customers, and industrial facilities to ARAMARK Corp. for approximately $800 million in November 2001,[16] thereby enabling the firm to reduce its long-term to a debt load to a more manageable $1.1 billion by the end of 2001.[17] This division had failed to achieve acceptable revenue growth rates and profitability levels. Among other divestitures, ServiceMaster sold its commercial landscape construction business, its continental European pest control and property services operations, and its pest-elimination business in the United Kingdom and Ireland.[18]

Returning to its domestic American, on-location roots, ServiceMaster today operates three units: lawn care; maintenance and improvement; and termite and pest control.[19] First, it is the leading provider in the United States of residential and commercial lawn, tree, and shrub services under the names of TruGreen ChemLawn and LandCare, through 201 company-owned and sixty-four franchised TruGreen ChemLawn locations and 132 LandCare locations.

Second, the firm provides maintenance and improvement services. It offers cleaning services under the name Merry Maids. The unit is the leading provider of house cleaning services in the United States, through fifty-eight company-owned and 754 franchised locations. Another division, ServiceMaster Clean, is the leading U.S. franchisers of residential and commercial cleaning services through a network of nearly 3,000 franchisees. It also offers: plumbing, electrical heating and air conditioning services under the names American Residential Services through seventy company-owned locations and American Mechanical Services (for commercial customers) through fifteen company-owned locations; home systems and appliance warranty contracts under the name American Home Shield, a leading provider of these contracts in the United States; and home inspection services under the name AmeriSpec, a leading provider of these services in the United States through three company-owned and 223 franchised locations.

Third, ServiceMaster offers residential and commercial termite and pest control services under the name Terminix, the leading provider of these services in the United States, through 318 company-owned and 134 franchised locations.

Ward sought to restructure ServiceMaster as an umbrella organization focusing mainly, but not exclusively, on residential services, providing individuals and dual-income families with one-stop shopping in the above three areas, using the power of national brands to reassure existing and potential customers.[20] It wants to offer services for everything a homeowner needs, but is too busy (or unwilling) to do. In particular, its units serve two-career, middle and upper-middle income, time-starved families, by undertaking tasks that people neither have the time nor the desire to do themselves. Those in a time bind do not want, for example, to deal with the typical problems of independent maids—green cards, backaches, and child care. These become the concerns of a local franchisee or company office. Furthermore, mobile employees find the same standardized, branded services wherever they relocate in the United States. Another key market is an aging population that needs assistance with maintaining yards and keeping homes clean.

The firm has emphasized cross-selling and synergies, for instance, striving to "move" its pest control customers into its lawn care or maid (or both) services.[21] Its division share lists and refer customers to each other. Employee uniforms sport a universal logo in an effort to build a company-wide brand name.

After the acquisition of the Terminix and Merry Maids units, ServiceMaster initiated its Quality Services Network in 1989 to bring the range of its residential consumer services to the attention of potential customers. It created a toll-free telephone number, staffed by cross-trained operators to connect current and potential customers to the full range of the firm's home services providers. Potential cross-sell customers could call its 800-number to obtain referrals for service providers in their locales. In turn, local service providers received these leads and the opportunity to follow up. It also devised a coupon program offering discounts on its various consumer services. However, the Quality Services Network never lived up to management's expectations.

At the height of the e-commerce boom, ServiceMaster sought to revitalize its Quality Services Network by launching WeServeHomes.com in 2000. WeServeHomes.com, a separately organized joint venture between ServiceMaster and Kleiner, Perkins, Caufield & Byers, a venture capital firm, represented the first internet provider offering homeowners the opportunity to obtain multiple residential services from one online destination. It subcontracted the delivery of services to ServiceMaster units or others where no ServiceMaster units offered services. However, in 2002, the firm recognized a failure and buried this e-commerce idea, continuing online operations at its corporate website, ServiceMaster.com, and providing Yahoo! customers with the ability to schedule and buy residential services through Yahoo! Home Service Center.[22]

Cross-selling represents, however, a challenge. Among affluent, dual-income families, each spouse may be responsible for different home services. Cross-selling to these couples requires marketing to both spouses. However, it is often difficult to get spouses together during weekdays to market to them. Because the ServiceMaster brand remained subordinated to its various business units, customers did not know of the interrelationship of these entities. Customers may also resist calling one source for different homecare services that typically are purchased and delivered separately, with divergent expertise, equipment, and frequencies.

Religious Orientation of the Firm's Leaders

Wade's evangelical orientation began when he was "reborn" at the age of thirty-two, at the Moody Church in Chicago, one of the nation's most prominent pulpits of Christian fundamentalism.[23] He made a declaration for Jesus, a deliberate and conscious acceptance of Jesus as his personal Savior.[24] Wade sought to bear witness to his rebirth by applying the Bible to his daily conduct. He wanted to live his faith and values throughout the week. A later "precipitating crisis" revived his commitment.

After nearly going blind in a 1944 accident, when chemicals used to annihilate moths exploded in his face, Wade rededicated himself to God. He came to believe that running a profitable business was not inconsistent with serving God. Wade recalled:

> I found myself wondering what the Lord would do with a company that was entirely His, a company in which every employee, from top to bottom, did his job for the glory of God....
>
> I closed my eyes and I prayed. I told the Lord that I loved Him and that I trusted in His love for the foregiveness of my neglects. I pledged that there and then I was committing myself to Him entirely—myself, my homes, my business—day and night. I would turn everything over to Him.[25]

In thus pledging himself to God, Wade stated, "[B]ut I want You [God] to tell me how to run things and to send my way the men I need to do the job. I realize that all I have to know is in the Bible and I will seek it, but I will need Your help to understand it. I choose to serve the Lord, but You will have to show me how."[26] Reflecting an inner calm, characteristic of many modern evangelical business executives, such as Parker of Covenant Transport, Wade declared, "Whenever a problem of any kind comes up, I consult with Him [God] through prayer, meditation and the Bible. The decision is my own and I am responsible for it, but as long as I make it on His terms, I know I have nothing to worry about."[27] He further stated, "[I]f I run it [my business] in a way that honors the Lord, I won't have too much to worry about."[28]

Wade desired his commitment to God to be known, openly, in his firm and in the community. He stated, "I wanted to have men working with me who would know what the Lord had done, and was doing, because such men I knew that, as the Lord was receiving me into His glory, I would be able to tell Him that His company was still working for Him."[29]

When Wade returned to work, he told his employees about his commitment to God. He recalled, "As I expected, they joined me in it completely. Thereafter, we began each day with a prayer and an acknowledgment of our commitment. In honoring the Lord we knew that He would honor us if He were satisfied with us, and we sought nothing more."[30]

Wade and his employees continued to start each business day in prayerful commitment, submitting themselves to God and the Eternal's Will. According to Wade, he and his employees got along better; they were more willing to go the extra mile; they resolved their disagreements through prompt and open discussion, rather than carrying grudges or losing their tempers. A dedication to God and to the Eternal's Service, "brought vitality to the group [and]...a new pride in doing a good job."[31]

As the firm's senior executive, Wade saw that his first responsibility was to conduct business "along lines that will be pleasing to the Lord."[32] For Wade, each of us should serve God by using the Bible, which he regarded as divinely authored, as the handbook for our relations with others. Believing that the Bible is God talking to us,[33] Wade stated, "The Bible is a practical guide to Christian living. It contains the Lord's counsel for all the problems that face us, and it is addressed to those who are specifically seeking that counsel."[34]

Proper use of the Bible for Wade involved not only making a commitment to God, but also surrendering to scriptural precepts. He devoted himself to "the unreserved application of those precepts, the complete turning over to God of one's life—at home, on the road, at the club, in the office.[35]

Wade saw his employees as masters of service who worked for the Lord; they were "good and faithful" servants of their Master— God.[36] According to Wade:

> We must become servants, servants first of all of the Lord and then, in His Name, servants unto all. We must serve. We must give service. Serving the Lord, we must give Him the only things He wants of us: our love and obedience. And we bear witness to this love and obedience by the type of service we give others. In business, the others are our stockholders, our boards, our staffs, our fellow businessmen, our competition and most of all, our customers....
>
> [I]f we ever hope to be able to recognize the guidance with which God has filled the Bible, we must decide here and now that we are going to be good and faithful servants and, like Paul, ask Him: "Master, what would you have me do?" The answer will come in terms of what we must do for others, toward others and with others, and the answers are all in the Bible.[37]

Reflecting the biblical principle of stewardship in a business context, Wade noted, "A man is as accountable to God for his stewardship in the ministry of business as in the ministry of being a husband or a father."[38] Wade sought continual improvement in the firm and its operations so more people would be willing to do business with the company and more employees could fulfill their own potential.[39]

Even as the company grew, it remained Christian in perspective, with a "strong emphasis on Christianity."[40] Employees were still able to get together, despite their Christian denominational differences, in the company's conference room on Friday mornings to pray and sing together and enjoy the fellowship that made them a team.[41] Under Wade, the entity remained evangelical in its orientation. He maintained, "This is the way we at ServiceMaster ask the Lord to use our company—to help bring others to Him."[42]

Hansen, who succeeded Wade, looked to God, the Bible, and Jesus.[43] He saw that the chief aim of humanity was to glorify and enjoy God. Furthermore the Bible, as God's word, served as the primary means of knowing God, the place where Hansen met God "personally, directly." The life of Jesus enabled Hansen to grow in becoming "a man who glorifies and enjoys God in every area of life." Through his ServiceMaster work, Hansen applied "life in Christ" as well and as constantly as he could. He made God, through Jesus, the central focus of his life. Hansen ascribed his personal relationship to Jesus as giving "purpose, zest and motive power to life." Over the years, as he grew as a leader-manager, he became "committed to using work to help people develop rather than to use people to accomplish the work as the end." Service in business became for him service to God. He noted: "Our business is a gift from God to use as a vehicle to service Him by serving others."

Hansen practiced servant-leadership. Shortly after he retired as ServiceMaster's CEO, he was the after-dinner speaker at a firm meeting. As he waited to speak, he saw a server holding a large tray of desserts go toward a stand occupied by another tray. Hansen jumped up and removed the first tray, thereby assisting the server.[44]

After Hansen, Wessner assumed corporate leadership. Wessner also held firm to Wade's principles, noting, "Our company recognizes God's sovereignty in all areas of our business. Our objective is to apply consistently the principles, standards and values of the Bible in our business attitudes and actions."[45]

Echoing Wade, who felt that people were accountable to God for their stewardship in what he regarded as the ministry of a business, Wessner viewed the biblical concept of stewardship as the driving force for ServiceMaster.[46]

Wessner also emphasized the use of the firm's then expertise, namely, cleaning of healthcare facilities, in additional markets, such as educational institutions, rather than developing new areas of expertise. Like John Beckett profiled in chapter 8, he felt a strong sense of limits with respect to what the company could successfully do. Under Wessner, ServiceMaster pursued growth within the context of the company's established business sphere.[47]

Under Wessner's leadership, the firm formulated and first used in 1973 the four core values that continue to serve as the company's foundation. ServiceMaster has long declared that its primary goal is "to honor God in all we do." This serves as a constant reminder for the firm and all of its employees to do the right thing in the right way. Its three other objectives are: "To help people develop; To pursue excellence; To grow profitably."[48] These key values provide the "ethic for the firm, or way of seeking to do what is right and avoiding what is wrong...., a moral reference point, a compass heading that provides guidance for the way things are done."[49]

The four corporate values were so important to the firm that they were chiseled into a curving marble wall stretching ninety feet long and standing eighteen feet tall at its headquarters building in the Chicago suburb of Downers Grove, Illinois.[50] Carved prominently in the stone letters nearly one foot high were four statements so that every headquarters employee could know these values and strive to live by them. In 2002, the company moved the marble inscription to its consumer services division training facility in Memphis, Tennessee.

Reflecting on the first two of its four corporate values, Wessner stated, "We believe that God has created all things and that we honor [H]im when we honor [H]is creation. We do that when we create an environment in our business dealings that will help people—whether our own employees or the people we serve—to become all that God has intended them to be.... It is a spiritual motivation."[51] Profit for Wessner was not "an end in itself. It is a means to accomplish our other objectives."[52] Thus, he emphasized employee development and satisfaction believing that they led to enhanced motivation and a higher level of service quality, in turn, leading to greater customer satisfaction, enhanced profits, and the ability to develop new personnel,[53] topics examined later in this chapter.

As the top executive at ServiceMaster, Wessner squarely faced the conflict between a self-denying Christian concern for others and the hoped for financial returns for the business he headed. However, he was able to make difficult business decisions in the context of the firm's long-term success. With many contracts in place, he built in a degree of financial slack, allowing him to make difficult decisions without the company being forced into a precarious financial position or a survival mode.

For example, Wessner on occasion faced a conflict between his Christian values and an important business opportunity.[54] ServiceMaster had taken over a significant hospital-cleaning contract. The hospital's chief administration was a very harsh and difficult person, who had a drinking problem and a bad temper; he used unacceptable language and abused his own staff. The ServiceMaster manager in charge went to Wessner and expressed his concern for the firm's staff. Agreeing that it was unfair for the company's people to work in such a personally abusive situation, Wessner cancelled the contract, viewing it as inconsistent with the organization's philosophy of employee development.

The leadership of ServiceMaster next turned to Pollard. In the mid 1990s, he wrote a best selling book, *The Soul of the Firm*, offering his theories about mixing God and profits. Pollard stated:Profit is a means in God's world to be used and invested, not an end to be worshiped.

> Profit is a legitimate measurement of the value of our effort. It is an essential source of capital....
> God and business do mix, and profit is a standard for determining the effectiveness of our combined efforts.... It is the leader's responsibility to manage within the firm to produce profit. For us, the common link between God and profit is people.[55]

Pollard also asserted: "People and profits are part of our mission. Profit is how we are measured by our owners. It provides the resources to grow and develop people."[56]

Looking the servant-leadership provided by Jesus, as discussed in chapter 2, Pollard maintained that "even the humblest of tasks is worthy for a leader to do." He continued, "There certainly is no scarcity of feet to wash, and towels are always available. I suggest that the only limitation, if there is one, involves the ability of each of us as leaders to be on our hands and knees, to compromise our pride, to be involved, and to have compassion for those we serve."[57]

Living his faith and being an example to others, Pollard led by serving others, never asking anyone to do something he was unwilling to do himself. At one board meeting, Pollard, then board chairman, having spilt coffee on the boardroom carpet just prior to the meeting, went down on his hands and knees to clean up the mess he created. Also, according to one observer, the firm's directors, while conversing over breakfast, hardly appeared to notice Pollard's actions. At ServiceMaster, a leader was expected to serve.[58]

Continuing ServiceMaster's longstanding orientation, Pollard saw the company's more spiritual engagement in terms of the respect for each individual's worth and dignity and a commitment to employee development. According to Pollard, "At ServiceMaster, we have chosen to build our objectives on the conclusion that we live in God's world, and that every individual has been created in God's image with dignity and worth. It is where we begin as we try to determine the right way to run our business."[59]

Accepting and facilitating the development of the different people whom God created, Pollard concluded, reflecting the beliefs of his mentor, Max DePree, that "a key to success in developing the soul of your firm is to harness the power of diversity."[60] He stated, reflecting a more inclusive, spiritual-orientation, "We can't and shouldn't and don't want to drive people to a particular religious belief. But we do want people to ask the fundamental questions. What's driving them? What is this life all about?"[61] Under Pollard, ServiceMaster became an inclusive organization, accepting religious and other differences among its employees.[62] As CEO, Pollard saw his daily challenge not just to talk about his faith, but as he put it, "to live my faith in the way I recognize and treat others, including those who do not agree with me or my faith."[63]

Although Pollard's book encapsulated the firm's long-standing policies, he saw, perhaps more clearly than Wade or Wessner, the creative tension between the firm's basic principles, namely, honoring God and helping people develop, which he regarded as end goals, and the two means goals, the pursuit of excellence and the need to grow profitably.[64] Yet for Pollard, the firm's four values provided "a checkpoint or early warning signal that helps us understand the direction we are headed."[65]

Today, Jonathan Ward, its current top executive, seeks to build on the steps taken by Pollard and to refocus ServiceMaster in a spiritually oriented direction. Ward has emphasized the concept of servant-leadership. For him, servant leadership connotes leading as one wishes to be led. It means, "[W]e're going to do it in a way that recognizes the human dignity of every person—which means we will develop people as we deliver results." He continued, "As a leader I'm highly aware that my life touches many lives. I want to build an enterprise where servant-leadership is the model of how we interact with one another."[66]

At the same time, expressing his religious beliefs, Ward indicated "For me, God is real. My personal faith has as its center Jesus Christ, [W]ho challenges me to be more like [H]im—to use [H]is life as an example—to live in service to others." Yet, Ward also noted, "I respect and encourage deep faith. Whether it is a Christian, Jew, Muslim, Buddhist or Hindu—I strive to ensure that they are welcome at ServiceMaster."[67] Putting the firm's commitment to God in a new, non-evangelistic light, Ward concluded, "If you have a faith, bring it in. We don't expect you to be converting people to your faith, but we're going to welcome your whole being, the whole of you as an individual, everything about you."[68]

Religion does not figure into ServiceMaster's current employment practices. As Pollard stated, "[A]t ServiceMaster we never allow religion or the lack thereof to become a basis for exclusion or how we treat each other professionally or personally."[69] Carlos H. Cantu, an evangelical Mexican-American who came up the ranks at Terminix and served as ServiceMaster's chief executive officer from 1994 to 1999 and as its senior chairman from 1999 to 2001, put it this way, "We are an inclusive organization. We welcome and respect all nature of beliefs. The focus is on respect for the dignity and worth of individuals."[70] Today, ServiceMaster hires the followers of a variety of religious faiths, including Hindus and Muslims.[71] It pays its employees based on performance and promotes based on merit and potential.[72]

In other aspects of its operations, the firm now downplays its historic religious orientation. An eleven-foot statue of Jesus, washing the feet of a disciple, stood for a long period of time at the firm's suburban Chicago headquarters, before being moved in 2002 to the company's consumer services division training facility in Memphis.[73] Although some commentators had maintained that the statue served as a representation of an historic act of being a good and faithful servant, not solely as a religious symbol,[74] as one longtime ServiceMaster executive stated, "I don't know how you can believe that they're not throwing out the old stuff and the old ways. For God sakes, they're moving Jesus to Memphis."[75]

Since the late 1990s, the firm has moved away from offering numerous opportunities for Christian worship at its headquarters.[76] For many years, employees gathered for prayer and Bible study. Opportunities were offered to participate in Christian rituals at an on-site chapel. Racks offered evangelistic pamphlets by Wessner and Pollard. The firm also sponsored morning prayer sessions during Lent.[77] Although attendance at these groups and services was voluntary, some employees previously felt that their sponsorship by top management "put undo pressure on the employees to conform."[78]

Today, the firm makes space available for various employee-initiated religious groups to engage in prayer and scripture study. As its only current group worship activity, it sponsors a voluntary worship service each year for its headquarters employees on the president's National Day of Prayer.[79]

Vestiges of the old ServiceMaster remain, however. Although a publicly held corporation, its annual reports contain biblical verses.[80] Shareholder meetings begin with prayer. Continuing the firm's tradition, Ward calls meetings to order with biblical quotes, such as those from the Book of Isaiah.[81] Others begin meetings with a devotional, a prayer, a meditation, or an inspirational thought to enable attendees to take a deep breath and think about the scope of their lives, before turning to the matters at hand.[82]

ServiceMaster's Employee-Focus

Throughout its long history, ServiceMaster put its employees and their development behind only being servants to God. As a low tech service firm, whether through its consumer services units or its former management services division, it applied its expertise in buying up and consolidating (in modern business terms, rolling up) cottage industries and then operating labor-intensive businesses and managing them well. Over the years, its top executives realized that the firm's success and profitability depended (and continues to depend) on satisfied customers. Simply put, dispirited, uncommitted, unengaged, and untrained employees could not generate the requisite customer satisfaction. Thus, the firm's goal is "to grow people—to train, to equip, and to motivate people to be more effective in their work."[83]

ServiceMaster's corporate credo emphasizes valuing employees at every level and treating them with respect, based on the dignity and worth of each employee created in God's image and each human's potential to achieve.[84] As Wade put it, "In a company dedicated to the Lord every employee can have this same feeling of vital membership [based on the notion that everyone is of equal value], and it is more than attitude. It is a fact." At ServiceMaster, Wade continued, "We are very much aware of this fact."[85] Furthermore, he saw a corporate executive as a steward for his employees because "as boss his personal worth to the business will be judged largely on the basis of his ability to help people grow."[86]

Reflecting the importance of its employees, based on the "belief that people are special,"[87] Pollard sought to align the firm's mission with each employee's personal growth and development. In striving to make each task personally satisfying and rewarding, he spun out the "process of doing and becoming" based on eight points: first, the value of each person as an individual with unique skills and talents; second, the recognition of the benefit and reality of diversity; third, harnessing the power of a common purpose: fourth, the encouragement of employee empowerment, ownership, and accountability; fifth, the recognition that learning is a lifelong experience; sixth, the demand for service by the example of the firm's leaders; and eighth, the acceptance of and building on the abilities of ordinary people and the expectation of extraordinary performance.[88]

Behind its efforts rests a hardheaded reality. ServiceMaster sought to increase the productivity and the quality of service provided by its low-paid employees, doing menial and repetitive tasks, such as killing bugs or providing maid service, by offering them respect and a sense of dignity, so that each would perform up to his or her potential.[89] Channeling its "dignification effort into employee character traits," as Laura Nash concluded, would be good for the firm and capitalism."[90] Striving to give its employees the opportunity to develop and fulfill their potential enabled the firm to grow and become more profitable.

ServiceMaster's culture continues to focus on carefully selecting its employees, looking for people with a strong work ethic, a sense of responsibility and trustworthiness, and a service-oriented, caring characteristic. It then trains and motivates them, encouraging their growth and development. In asking the question, "What is your business?," management consultant extra ordinaire Peter Drucker told ServiceMaster's directors, "Your business is simply the training and development of people. You package it all different ways to meet the needs and demands of the customer, but your basic business is people training and motivation. You are delivering services. You can't deliver quality service to the customer without motivated and trained people."[91] According to Wessner, "We are in a business of training people. We train everyone from housekeeping aides to the chief operating officer. To grow, we had to have trained people who could relate to executives and housekeeping aides directly."[92] Teaching and learning thus became (and continues) as a key element of the company's business.

ServiceMaster achieves personal dignification through many forms of training, viewing development in broad terms. As Wessner noted, "At ServiceMaster, we invest a great deal of time and effort in education and training of people at every level of our company. The focus of this activity is not so much on what we want our people to do, but rather on what we want people to be."[93]

The firm still trains its employees meticulously in the requisite basic skills, such as, how to mop floors, previously through pictorial, color-coded teaching materials and now using videos.[94] Traditionally, it used a five-step teaching method for basic job skill training. A supervisor (or a team leader) performed and explained a task. Then, the leader asked the student to perform the task, with the leader providing coaching. The student then taught the task to the leader and another student. Finally, the teacher and the student learned how to inspect the work.[95]

A variety of broad-based training and educational programs, everything from remedial reading and language skills, to instruction in hygiene, the "social graces," and being civil to each other, also help employees improve their self-image, self-respect, self-development, and future prospects, thereby assisting them to "be something." Although many of its jobs are standardized and procedurally driven, for example, it allocates so much time for a team to clean a house, the firm strives to assist its employees in their growth and development, both personally and professionally. As Pollard put it, "At ServiceMaster, the task before us is to train and motivate people to serve so that they will do a more effective job, be more productive in their work, and yes, even be better people.... It is, in fact our mission.... The mission of our firm is understood to include the personal development and growth of that person as she or he serves others."[96]

Customer service also depends on employee motivation, based on the firm's mission and its core values. According to Pollard, "Every firm should be able to articulate a mission that reaches beyond the task and provides a hope that efforts and activities of its people are adding up to something significant—so significant, in fact, that even more can be accomplished than is expected."[97]

How does an employee find meaning and purpose in a mundane job, like cleaning a toilet? Pollard often used the example of Shirley, a hospital housekeeper. After fifteen years, she was still excited about her work. As Pollard explained:

When Shirley sees her task as extending to the patient in the bed and as an integral part of supporting the work of doctors and nurses, she has a cause—a cause that involves the health and welfare of others. She came to us no doubt, merely looking for a job, but she brought to us an unlocked potential and desire to accomplish something significant. She recently confirmed the importance of her cause when she told me, "If we don't clean with a quality effort, we can't keep the doctors and nurses in business; we can't accommodate patients. This place would be closed if we didn't have housekeeping."[98]

The firm's front-line workers, today, those who go into residences and commercial establishments, serve as the organization's eyes and ears. Thus, it trains them not only to do their tasks today, but also to look out for what the company and its various units could be doing in the future.[99]

ServiceMaster also strives to recognize its employees' efforts, thereby contributing to dignification. At its consumer services headquarters in Memphis, the firm sponsors an annual Employee Appreciation Day when employees are honored for their work through the granting of awards. The company also demonstrates its appreciation of its employees through a Pride Week, which also serves as an opportunity to show its employees what ServiceMaster now does, how large it is, and enables each division to educate other units as to what it does.[100]

Dignification also led the firm to achieve egalitarian goals through two means. First, for a number of years, no executive had a base compensation of more than twelve times the salary paid to an entry level manager.[101] Thus, in 1998, as president and CEO, Cantu received a base salary of $475,000.[102] The limitation on executive compensation ended with the recruitment Ward, an outsider, who received an annual base salary of not less 700,000 (paid in 2001 and increased to $725,000 in 2002). The firm's employment agreement with Ward also provides for annual incentive compensation, a grant of participation units under its Long-Term Performance Award Plan, stock options, loans including those to finance his purchase of ServiceMaster convertible debentures.[103]

Second, from the formation of Wade, Wenger & Associates, employees received the opportunity to buy shares in the firm and the chance to buy more shares whenever they wished.[104] Wade even went so far as to lend money to his employees so that they could buy stock in the entity.[105] As a public company, ServiceMaster instituted an employee share purchase plan thereby encouraging its personnel to participate as shareholders in the profits they generated.[106] Today, all full-time employees have the opportunity to buy shares under this plan with about 20 percent currently owning stock in the corporation.[107] As a result of the firm's rapid expansion, employees own about 15 percent of the firm's stock, a smaller proportion than in the past.[108]

The egalitarian theme carries over into the managerial training and work in the field. The firm's managerial training program requires future managers to participate in front-line, on-location jobs, spending a period of time doing the task he or she will supervise. According to Wessner, "[A] manager who hasn't personally experienced what it's like to wear a green uniform and be treated as a nonperson can never fully understand the importance of his or her responsibility to see that all employees are treated with dignity and to make certain that the job itself is dignifying."[109]

Pollard, who joined the company as a senior vice president, had as his first job assignment the task of working with the housekeeping, operations, and maintenance teams at a hospital, cleaning patient rooms, including bathrooms and toilets. This assignment enabled him to see firsthand how others treat and view those who serve in menial capacities.[110] As he recalled:

> I was working in a busy corridor of the hospital. I had just set out my wet-floor signs and was about to mop the floor. People were streaming back and forth when suddenly a lady stopped and asked, "Aren't you Bill Pollard?" I responded that I was, and she identified herself as a distant relative of my wife. Then she looked at me and my mop, shook her head, and asked, "Aren't you a lawyer?" as if to say, "Can't you get a better job?" I paused, looked down at my bucket, and said, "No, I have a new job." By this time several other people had gathered around. She was now embarrassed and leaned close to me and whispered, "Is everything all right at home?"[111]

Even after the completion of a training program, every manager, at its corporate and divisional headquarters as well as its company-owned and franchise locations, regardless of his or her position, must spend at least one day a year, a We Serve Day, working in the field, providing one of the firm's services to its customers. Requiring managers to spend one day a year in the trenches puts them closer to the company's employees and customers, making them more open to hearing their ideas and needs.[112]

ServiceMaster also expects its managers to devote a significant percentage of their time to nurturing and developing employees. Managers provide quarterly people-development reports on each employee. Managerial compensation takes into account how their decisions and actions reflect the four key corporate values.[113]

Employers of the working poor face a familiar litany, namely, unreliable transportation, childcare problems, and health difficulties, that manifest themselves in employee unreliability, ultimately leading to discharge, and increased turnover. However, most ServiceMaster employees feel good about their unskilled, low-paying positions. Prior to the sale of its management services division, ServiceMaster's employee turnover rate was enviably low. It enjoyed a 14 percent to 20 percent turnover rate among its non-seasonal employees, compared with about 30 percent for comparable positions in the industry.[114]

Looking Behind the Noble Image

ServiceMaster proudly proclaimed in its 1995 Annual Report, under the heading "Quality is Truth":

> Our philosophy of doing business starts with the belief that people are created in God's image, with dignity and worth; that service cannot be delivered without people; and that quality service cannot be delivered without motivated and trained people.
> This foundation of belief challenges US to serve with integrity and adherence to standards of truth and honesty.
> Quality and truth are both important. They are, to us, the reality of doing what we say. Our customers expect extraordinary service—performance that surpasses their expectations—and this is our pursuit of excellence.[115]

Over the last ten years or so, significant questions have arisen regarding ServiceMaster's commitment to excellence in its customer service. Despite being named as *Fortune* magazine's most admired outsourcing company in 1999 but dropping to third in this category the next year where it remains today,[116] the firm found it hard to live up to its saintly standards.

Terminix, its termite and pest-control unit, has run afoul of regulators in a number of states.[117] In 1999, the State of Connecticut sued Terminix for a number of violations, including allegedly operating without having an employee present who had the required supervisory pesticide-safety certification, failing to give adequate written instructions for spraying pesticides, and falsifying pesticide application records.[118] Ultimately, in 2002, Terminix agreed to pay the State of Connecticut $1 million to settle the three-year legal battle over thousands of alleged violations of the state's pesticide laws.[119] In the settlement, Terminix made not admission of law or fact and expressly denied all alleged violations of law. In addition to reforming its business practices and instituting an audit program to ensure compliance with state pesticide rules, Terminix agreed not to open any new offices in the state for two years as well as to temporarily close one branch office and not to accept new business there for one year. When the office reopened, the parent corporation, ServiceMaster, was required, under the settlement, to supervise the office for one year thereafter.

In 2001, a former branch manager of a Terminix office in Mineola, Long Island, servicing Queens, Nassau, and Suffolk counties in New York State, pleaded guilty to defrauding customers by providing an insufficient amount of pesticides for termite treatments.[120] The plea came after inspectors from the New York State Department of Environmental Conservation had conducted a two-year study of the office and uncovered the falsification of pesticide application records, resulting in customers paying for treatments they did not receive. The investigation found that 65 percent of the 300 customers surveyed were under treated.

In a 1999 settlement with the Pennsylvania Department of Environmental Protection, Terminix agreed to change its termite treatment procedures statewide. The firm also agreed to pay penalties totaling $225,000 as a result of a severe fish kill in December 1997. The penalties were the largest ever assessed for a termiticide-related fish kill in Pennsylvania.[121]

Public officials have also accused Terminix of regularly failing to provide consumers with promised services. The State of Florida's settlement with Terminix in 1997 required refunds or retreatments to some 5,400 Floridians and the payment of a penalty to the state of $200,000 to cover investigation costs.[122] In 1994, Terminix entered into a consent judgment with the Kentucky Attorney General dealing with the firm's allegedly deceptive business practices concerning termite control services. A revised settlement in 1999 included remedying past problems, making contributions of $400,00 to Office of Attorney General Consumer Litigation and Education Fund and a Termite Entomology and Consumer Awareness Research Fund, and paying civil penalties of $267,000.[123] In 1995, Terminix also paid fines of $146,950 to the Commonwealth of Massachusetts to settle claims, including allegedly using unlicensed and uncertified workers to apply pesticides more than two thousand times.[124]

Today, a website, Terminix-Consumer Alert, exists. It posts complaints from consumers and employees as well as information about state investigations and lawsuit settlements against the Terminix and other ServiceMaster units.[125] Terminix sued to enjoin the website, alleging trademark infringement, but then withdrew its complaint.[126]

Regretting the lapses at Terminix, which he saw as "inevitable" given the number of employees (250,000) at the firm's company-owned and franchised locations, who service over ten million customers residential and commercial annually,[127] Pollard stated:

> People are human. They can and do make mistakes and sometimes do the wrong things. For the most part, our people are out serving in the customers' location without direct supervision. I know of no management system that can control all their actions. The issue is what is in their heart as well as what is in their head. The challenge for us is to lead, train and motivate our people to serve, to do what is right, and to contribute to a nurturing and caring environment—that is what our corporate objectives are all about. When we fail, we must be open about our shortcomings, take corrective action, seek forgiveness, and strive for improvement. Failure can be a learning experience. At the end of the day, the implementation of our objectives, and the combined result of our leadership and service, must benefit the customer; otherwise, we have not done our job.[128]

Upon becoming the CEO in 2001, Ward saw a mounting sense of urgency to solve the problems that undermined customer satisfaction. Prior to Ward, there was "a belief that excessive measurement activity and formal control hurt the spirit of the organization, and that excessive monitoring betray[ed] a counterproductive lack of trust in subordinates' competence and behavior."[129] However, Ward recognized the need to train ServiceMaster's managers and personnel across the board (not just those at Terminix) in better methods to eliminate errors and defects that otherwise would result in poor customer service. The company turned to Six Sigma, a quality measurements and business improvement technique.[130] It is also a methodology to drive and shape business strategy, so that an enterprise remains viable and profitable.

Six Sigma, as customer-oriented, data-driven technique focusing on analyzing and solving root causes of business problems, aims for quality improvements. At an operational level, it strives to shrink process variation and avoid defects in goods or services that negatively affect customers. In other words, if properly implemented, it reduces defects, improves processes, enhances customer satisfaction, and decreases costs. Although originally applied to manufacturing processes, Six Sigma provides tools to enable a firm to improve any type of process.

Six Sigma starts with the customer. It asks what do customers want, defines key customer requirements, and then delivers with as little variation as possible from their expectations. As a process improvement tool to meet customer needs and reduce product defects, the implementation of Six Sigma involves five steps embodied in the acronym DMAIC. The first three steps involve: defining customer needs and improvement goals, measuring the current process and its variably, and then analyzing the collected data to see where a process fails to deliver. The fourth step focuses on improving the process to fix the problem and achieve the performance goals. The last step consists of controlling (or monitoring) the improvements in the key variables to sustain the goals and ensure that the problem does not recur.

Six Sigma originated at Motorola, Inc. in 1984 and found its best-known application in the firm's Bandit pager, a superior designed and manufactured product. Motorola's innovators adopted sigma, the Greek letter indicating a deviation from an accepted outcome, as the moniker for the new technique. Six Sigma measures a process in terms of defects. The higher the sigma number, the lower the number of errors. At the Six Sigma level a process is working nearly perfectly, if not more than 3.4 bad customer experiences occur for every million customer opportunities.

But, Six Sigma is more than a statistical concept measuring various processes in terms of defects, it is also a management philosophy focusing on identifying errors and taking the action necessary to reduce them. The initial Six Sigma projects at ServiceMaster centered on determining the critical customer requirements for each customer base within its various units and on enhancing customer satisfaction through increased effectiveness and, at the same time, attaining enhanced efficiencies.[131]

In addition to measuring and improving customer satisfaction, Six Sigma also measures important operating metrics and holds managers accountable for improvements in these metrics, thereby helping profitability. An organization determines the success of a Six Sigma program by calculating meaningful and sustainable costs savings or revenue increases. For example, at ServiceMaster, the introduction of Six Sigma in the spring of 2002 led to $200,000 in enterprise-wide savings by reducing long distance telephone calls (among other telecommunications savings), cutting uniform costs by $100,000, and slashing office supply expenditures.[132]

In pioneering the application of Six Sigma to a service business, Ward sought to tie improving the quality of employee performance and raising the level of existing consumer satisfaction and retention to concrete financial results. Furthermore, he asserted that Six Sigma serves as "the cornerstone of our transformation in both our operational performance and our culture. Our secret weapon is to take small gains and create big wins through the replication of hundreds of locations across the country."[133]

Business organizations also use Six Sigma to invigorate a firm's strategic planning process and as a technique to achieve specified objectives. ServiceMaster embraced Six Sigma as part of a strategy to enhance customer recognition of the firm's name and (that of its various units) as a provider of numerous, valuable household services. It seeks to use the process as a means to build a national brand name, well known for reliable services. In other words, returning to the cross-selling approach, discussed earlier in this chapter, ServiceMaster is striving to build an umbrella brand through delivering excellent customer service throughout and across all of its many residential service offerings.[134]

It remains to be seen whether the firm will succeed in meeting, or even exceeding, the service expectations of its customers and building a premium, national brand name. However, ServiceMaster did not suppress what was going on. Although maintaining that inconsistent interpretations of state rules and statutes as well as disagreement between federal and state rules about pesticide applications, for example, among other legal details, resulted in its compliance difficulties, ServiceMaster's top executives openly talked about customer dissatisfaction and sought to deal with the problem.[135] The firm followed its longstanding practice of having its mistakes "flushed out in the open for correction."[136]

* * *

In the early years of the twenty-first century, we can only conjecture about the impact of ServiceMaster's turning away from Wade's devotion to honoring God and promoting evangelical Christianity to become an inclusive, more spiritual business organization. Similar to many other corporations, the firm recognized the need to be more consumer-focused to ensure its survival and continued success. Under a modern CEO, it implemented the Six Sigma process, rather than looking to biblical principles, as Wade and others would likely have done.

Notes

1. Marion E. Wade with Glenn D. Kittler, *The Lord is My Counsel: A Businessman's Personal Experiences with the Bible* (Englewood Cliffs, NJ: Prentice-Hall 1966), 1-2.
2. Ibid., 99-100.
3. Ibid., 96-98.
4. Randall Balmer, *Encyclopedia of Evangelicalism* (Louisville, KY: Westminster John Knox, 2002), 613.
5. ServiceMaster L.P., 1994 Annual Report, 7.
6. Ibid.
7. Laura L. Nash, *Believers in Business* (Nashville, TN: Thomas Nelson, 1994), 110.
8. James L. Heskett, "Lessons in the Service Sector," *Harvard Business Review* 87:2 (March-April 1987): 118-126, at 122.
9. I have drawn on James L. Heskett, "ServiceMaster: We Serve," Harvard Business School Case Study, Boston, MA, N9-900-030 (June 6, 2000), 12-13 (Exhibit 3 Acquisitions and Divestitures, The ServiceMaster Company, 1986-1999); The ServiceMaster Co., Annual Report 2001, 41; ServiceMaster, 2000 Annual Report, 67-68; ServiceMaster, U.S. Securities and Exchange Commission (SEC) Form 10-K for Fiscal Year Ended December 31, 1999 (March 27, 2000), 28, 39; ServiceMaster, 1999 Annual Report, 3, 16, 27, 40; ServiceMaster, Prospectus Supplement (August 6, 1999), S-3; ServiceMaster, SEC Form 10-K for Fiscal Year Ended December 31, 1998 (March 29, 1999) 40-41; ServiceMaster, 1998 Annual Report, 2, 29, 41-42; Service Master SEC Form 10-K for Fiscal Year Ended December 31, 1997 (March 27, 1998), 2; ServiceMaster, 1997 Annual Report, 3, ServiceMaster, 1994 Annual Report, 34; ServiceMaster Co., SEC Form 10-Q (August 18, 1992), 7.
10. The ServiceMaster Co., 2000 Annual Report, 73.
11. David Barboza, "In This Company's Struggle, God Has Many Proxies," *New York Times*, November 21, 2001, C1, C6.
12. The ServiceMaster Co., 2002 Annual Report, 33.
13. William Blair & Co., "The ServiceMaster Co." (June 13, 2002), 2.
14. The ServiceMaster Co., 2002 Annual Report, 50; ServiceMaster, SEC Form 10-K for Fiscal Year Ended December 31, 2000, 5; ServiceMaster, 2000 Annual Report, 12, 70-71; ServiceMaster, SEC Form 10-K for Fiscal Year Ended December 31, 1999, 4, 40; ServiceMaster 1999 Annual Report, 41.
15. Linda A. Moore, "ServiceMaster to Focus on Consumer Units," *Commercial Appeal* (Memphis), October 5, 2001, C1.
16. The ServiceMaster Co., 2002 Annual Report, 28, 49; Service Master, SEC Form 10-K for Fiscal Year Ended December 31, 2001, 4; ServiceMaster, Annual Report 2001, 24, 39.
17. Ibid., 42. As of the end of 2002, its long-term debt had declined to $804 million. The ServiceMaster Co., 2002 Annual Report, 51.
18. The ServiceMaster Co., SEC Form 10-K for Fiscal Year Ended December 31, 2002 (March 31, 2003), 4; ServiceMaster, 2002 Annual Report, 48-49; ServiceMaster, SEC Form 10-K for Fiscal Year Ended December 31, 2001, 4; ServiceMaster, Annual Report 2001, 24, 39-40; ServiceMaster, SEC Form 10-K for Fiscal Year Ended December 31, 2000, 5.
19. The ServiceMaster Co., SEC Form 10-K for Fiscal Year Ended December 31, 2002, 1-3. Linda A. Moore, "Terminix Evolves with the Times," *Commercial Appeal* (Memphis), October 13, 2002, G1, provides a brief history of Terminix.

20. The ServiceMaster Co., 2000 Annual Report, 26, 28.
21. I have drawn on The ServiceMaster Co., 2000 Annual Report, 3; Heskett, "ServiceMaster," 7; Roger Hallowell, "WeServeHomes. com," Harvard Business School Case Study, Boston, MA, N9-802-004 (June 27, 2001), 11.
22. Ibid., 4-10; The ServiceMaster Co., 2000 Annual Report, 8, 43; ServiceMaster 1999 Annual Report, 9; Barbara Rose, "Many Online Ventures Fall Back to Earth," *Chicago Tribune*, March 3, 2002, Business Section, 1; *Do-It-Yourself Retailing*, "ServiceMaster Ends Home Depot Test, Initiates Programs with Yahoo!," 181: 3 (September 1, 2002): 21.
23. Balmer, *Encyclopedia*, 389.
24. Wade, *Lord*, 33-36, 177.
25. Ibid., 82.
26. Ibid., 83.
27. Ibid., 87.
28. Ibid., 39.
29. Ibid., 83.
30. Ibid., 88.
31. Ibid., 89.
32. Ibid., 2.
33. Ibid., 4, 9.
34. Ibid., 5.
35. Ibid., 9
36. Ibid., 121.
37. Ibid. 45.
38. Ibid., 7.
39. Ibid., 129.
40. Barboza, "Company's Struggle," C1. See also Daniel Machalaba, "More Employees Are Seeking to Worship Job on the Job," *Wall Street Journal*, June 25, 2002, B1, B12.
41. Wade, *Lord*, 153.
42. Ibid., 158.
43. The quotes in this paragraph are from Kenneth N. Hansen, *Reality* (Downers Grove, IL: The ServiceMaster Co., 1992), 7-10, 14.
44. Jonathan P. Ward, "The Advantage of Servant Leadership," in The ServiceMaster Co., Annual Report 2001, 20.
45. "As ServiceMaster's Chairman, Mr. Wessner Combined His Faith in God with a Strong Work Ethic," *Modern Healthcare* 22:37 (September 1992): 32-34, at 32, 34.
46. Nash, *Believers*, 103.
47. Ibid., 107.
48. See, e.g., ServiceMaster L.P., 1994 Annual Report, 3; C. William Pollard, *The Soul of the Firm* (Grand Rapids, MI: HarperBusiness and Zondervan, 1996), 18, 48, 129.
49. Ibid., 49. Also Ibid., 19.
50. Ibid., 18.
51. Nash, *Believers*, 103.
52. Ibid.
53. Ibid., 102.
54. Ibid., 117-118.
55. Pollard, *Soul*, 20.
56. Ibid., 18 (italics omitted).

57. Ibid., 130.
58. Heskett, "ServiceMaster," 2.
59. Pollard, *Soul*, 52 (italics omitted). Also Ibid., 21.
60. Ibid., 42; Telephone interview by author with C. William Pollard, January 29, 2003. Pollard has served on the board of directors of Herman Miller beginning in 1985. Herman Miller, Inc., SEC Schedule 14A, August 29, 2002, 11.
61. Marc Gunther, "God & Business," *Fortune* 144:1 (July 9, 2001): 58-80, at 64.
62. Pollard Interview; Pollard, *Soul*, 19-21, 41, 52, 119.
63. Pollard, *Soul*, 21.
64. Ibid., 48.
65. Ibid., 49. Also Ibid., 19.
66. Ward, "Servant Leadership," 20-21.
67. Ibid., 21.
68. Linda A. Moore, "Clean House."
69. Pollard, *Soul*, 20-21.
70. Dewanna Lofton, "Are You Being Fully Served?," *Commercial Appeal* (Memphis), October 4, 1998, C1. For background on Cantu, see Laurel Campbell, "Discipline, Faith Made Winner," *Commercial Appeal* (Memphis), April 20, 1997, Business Section, C1; Donna Chavez, "No Challenge Has Been Too Great for Carlos Cantu," *Chicago Tribune*, May 19, 1996, Tempo Section, D1.
71. Machalaba, "More Employees," B12; Calmetta Y. Coleman, "Religious Roots Sprout Divine Results at ServiceMaster," *Wall Street Journal*, September 12, 1995, B4.
72. Pollard, *Soul*, 36.
73. Ibid., 32; Telephone Interview by Matthew Mantel, Reference Librarian, The Jacob Burns Law Library, The George Washington University Law School with Kathy Lazar, Project Coordinator for Corporate Communications, The ServiceMaster Co., November 18, 2002.
74. Laurent Belsie, "Businesses That Build Foundations on Faith," *Christian Science Monitor*, January 24, 2000, 16.
75. Barboza, "Company's Struggle," C6.
76. Lazar Interview.
77. Edward C. Baig, "Profiting With Help From Above," *Fortune* 115:8 (April 27, 1987): 36-46, at 38; Nash, *Believers*, 250.
78. Ibid.
79. Lazar Interview; Telephone Interview by author with Steven Bono, Senior Vice president, Corporate Communications, The ServiceMaster Co., January 31, 2003. For the White House observance of the National Day of Prayer see Dana Milbank, "The National Day of Prayer," *Washington Post*, May 3, 2002, A6.
80. The ServiceMaster Co., 2000 Annual Report, back cover; ServiceMaster, 1999 Annual Report, inside front cover.
81. Barboza, "Company's Struggle," C1.
82. Bono Interview.
83. Pollard, *Soul*, 57.
84. Ibid., 22, 52, 57, 106.
85. Wade, *Lord*, 131.
86. Ibid., 144.
87. Pollard, *Soul*, 53 (italics omitted).
88. Ibid., 22.
89. Ronald Henkoff, "Service Is Everybody's Business," *Fortune* 129:13 (June 27, 1994): 48-60, at 60; David E. Bowen and Edward E. Lawler III, "Empowering Service Employees," *Sloan Management Review* 36 (Summer 1995): 73-84, at 79.

90. Nash, *Believers*, 134.
91. Pollard, *Soul*, 113.
92. "As ServiceMaster's Chairman," at 34.
93. ServiceMaster Co., 1997 Annual Report, 19. See also, Nash, *Believers*, 102, 137.
94. Ronald Henkoff, "ServiceMaster: Piety, Profits, and Productivity," *Fortune* 125:13 (June 29, 1992): 84-85, at 84.
95. Pollard, *Soul*, 115.
96. ServiceMaster Co., 1997 Annual Report, 20. See also Pollard, *Soul*, 129.
97. Ibid., 46.
98. Ibid., 46-47 (italics omitted).
99. Noel M. Tichy with Eli Cohen, *Leadership Engine: How Winning Companies Build Leaders at Every Level* (New York: HarperBusiness, 1997), 18-19.
100. Pollard, *Soul*, 58-59; Telephone Interview by Matthew Mantel, Reference Librarian, The Jacob Burns Law Library, The George Washington University Law School with Tim Anderson, Director of People Service, ServiceMaster Clean, December 11, 2002.
101. Robert A. Davis, "ServiceMaster Chief Focuses on Putting Employees First," *Chicago Sun-Times*, July 15, 1996, Financial Section, 45.
102. The ServiceMaster Co., SEC Schedule 14A (March 27, 2000), 19.
103. The ServiceMaster Co., SEC Schedule 14A (April 16, 2003), 27; Compensation and Leadership Development Committee Report on Executive Compensation and Agreements with Officers and Directors, Ibid., 24-26, 32; ServiceMaster, SEC Schedule 14A (March 22, 2002), 17; Compensation and Leadership Development Committee Report on Executive Compensation and Agreements with Officers and Directors, Ibid., 14-16, 20. Jonathan P. Ward's Employment Agreement, January 9, 2001, is set forth in the ServiceMaster Form 10K/A for Fiscal Year Ended December 31, 2000 (March 29, 2001), Exhibit 10.19.
104. Wade, *Lord*, 100, 120.
105. Tichy, *Leadership Engine*, 109.
106. Nash, *Believers*, 151; Pollard, *Soul*, 29.
107. Ibid., Gunther, "God & Business," at 64; Davis, "ServiceMaster Chief."
108. Heskett, "ServiceMaster" 4-5; Pollard, *Soul*, 104.
109. Nash, *Believers*, 137.
110. Pollard, *Soul*, 55.
111. Ibid., 14-15.
112. Ibid., 54; Lazar Interview.
113. Davis, "ServiceMaster Chief."
114. Davis, "ServiceMaster Chief;" Gillian Flynn, "Attracting the Right Employees— and Keeping Them," *Personnel Journal* 73:12 (December 1994): 44-49, at 46; Joseph A. Maciariello, "Management Systems at ServiceMaster," in *Faith in Leadership: How Leaders Live Out Their Faith in Their Work—and Why It Matters*, eds. Robert Banks and Kimberly Powell (San Francisco, CA: Jossey-Bass, 2000), 207-208. See also "How to Fill Thankless Jobs in a Tight Labor Market," *Business Week* 3718 (February 5, 2001) 30B-30D, at 30B.
115. ServiceMaster L.P., 1994 Annual Report, 3.
116. *Fortune*, "Where Companies Rank in Their Own Industries," 139:4 (March 1, 1999): F1-F7, at F2; *Fortune*, "Where Companies Rank In Their Industries," 141:4 (February 21, 2000): F-1-F-7, at F-6; *Fortune*, "Who's On Top and Who Flopped," 145:5 (March 4, 2002): 75-82, at 77; *Fortune*, "The Champs: Where Companies Rank In Their Industries," 147:4 (March 3, 2003): 87-94, at 89.

117. Gunther, "God & Business," at 64. ServiceMaster's lawncare unit has not been without its problems. For example, in 1999, TruGreen paid $600,000 to settle alleged violations of New York State pesticide laws, with $200,000 of the fine suspended in return for TrueGreen reducing its pesticide use in the state by five percent. Under the settlement, the firm agreed to implement more extensive notification requirements in its lawn postings and in its contracts with property owners. Fred O. Williams, "TrueGreen To Pay $600,000 Fine For Violating Pesticide Laws," *Buffalo News*, July 27, 1999, Section 6D.

118. Daniel P. Jones, "State Suing Terminix Over Alleged Violations," *Hartford Courant*, November 11, 1999, A3; *New York Times*, "Connecticut Sues Terminix," November 11, 1999, B13.

119. *In the Matter of Terminix International Co. L.P.* (Final Decision, Connecticut Department of Environmental Protection June 24, 2002) (Renewal of Business Registration Nos. B-0215, B-0372, and B-1140); Daniel P. Jones, "Terminix Agrees To Pay $1 Million," *Hartford Courant*, June 26, 2002, Connecticut Section, B5.

120. Press Release, Office of New York State Attorney General, Former Terminix Employee Pleads Guilty (April 10, 2001); Angelina Bonello, "Man Pleads Guilty in Pesticide Fraud," *Newsday*, April 11, 2001, A32.

121. *In the Matter of Terminix International Company L.P., Amwell Township, Washington County*, Pennsylvania Department of Environmental Protection (August 17, 1999) (Consent Order and Agreement); Press Release, Pennsylvania Department of Environmental Protection, Terminix Pays $225,000 Penalty for Severe Fish Kill (August 18, 1999).

122. *In the Matter of The Terminix International Company, L.P.*, Case No. 95-410099 (Florida Attorney General, Department of Legal Affairs, April 30, 1999) (Assurance of Voluntary Compliance); News Release, Florida Attorney General, Terminix to Offer Refunds, Retreatments for Termite Protection (April 30, 1997); Andy Miller, "Pest Control: Inside the Industry: A High Stakes Battle," *Atlanta Constitution*, September 28, 2000, Business Section, 1D.

123. *Commonwealth of Kentucky v Terminix International Corp.*, No. 94-CI 00745 (Franklin Circuit Court, Commonwealth of Kentucky, May 19, 1994) (Consent Judgment); *Commonwealth of Kentucky v Terminix International Corp.* (Franklin Circuit Court, Commonwealth of Kentucky, December 30, 1998) (Order Modifying Consent Judgment); Press Release, Kentucky Attorney General Announces $800,000 Terminix Settlement (January 4, 1999); Daniel P. Jones, "Exterminators Become Pests for Customers, *Hartford Courant*, July 12, 1999, A1.

124. *Commonwealth of Massachusetts v Terminix International Co. L.P.*, No. 92-7604-G, (Massachusetts Superior Court, November 10, 1995) (Settlement Agreement and Judgment).

125. The website is http://www.syix.com/emu/index.htm. See also Peter Spencer, "Consumer Revenge Dot Com," *Consumer's Research Magazine* 83:4 (April 2000): 43.

126. *Wall Street Journal*, "Terminix Drops Suit Against Operator of Site That Criticized Firm," March 13, 2000, A36; Rob Johnson, "Ex-Customer's Web Site Strings Terminix," *Commercial Appeal* (Memphis), February 27, 2000, A1.

127. Bono Interview; The ServiceMaster Co., 2002 Annual Report, 6.

128. Rich Hein, "ServiceMaster Co.: Firm In Spotlight For Pushing Its Workers to Care," *Chicago Sun-Times*, March 27, 2000, Financial Section, 52.

129. Maciariello, "Management Systems," at 212.

130. I have drawn on The ServiceMaster Co., 2002 Annual Report, 5; ServiceMaster, Annual Report 2001, 16, 25; Linda A. Moore, "ServiceMaster Lists Goals," *Commercial Appeal* (Memphis), April 27, 2002, Business Section, C8; Morgan Stanley,

"ServiceMaster Co." (April 25, 2002), 3. For background on Six Sigma, see George Eckes, *Six Sigma for Everyone* (Hoboken, NJ: John Wiley, 2003), 27-65; Greg Brue, *Six Sigma for Managers* (New York: McGraw-Hill, 2002), 1-35, 79-104. Dick Smith and Jerry Blakeslee with Richard Koonce, *Strategic Six Sigma: Best Practices from the Executive Suite* (Hoboken, NJ: John Wiley, 2002), offer a view of Six Sigma as a strategic tool for developing corporate strategy and facilitating organizational change.

131. Ibid., 27.
132. Ibid., 182.
133. Jonathan Ward, "Q2 2002 ServiceMaster Earnings Conference Call," July 30, 2002.
134. Smith and Blakeslee, *Strategic Six Sigma*, 27-28.
135. Pollard Interview; Bono Interview.
136. Pollard, *Soul*, 19. Also Ibid., 109.

6

Herman Miller, Inc.: A Transition from a Corporation Led by Evangelicals to a Secular Approach

For more than seven decades, a family of evangelicals, the DePrees, who pursued a progressive managerial approach, combining stewardship and servant-leadership styles, led Herman Miller to preeminence in the office furniture industry. When management passed out this family's hands, a new, secular CEO has continued to emphasize product, innovation, and environmental consciousness.

Business Background

The roots of Herman Miller go back to 1905, when the firm was founded as the Star Furniture Co., a maker of high-quality reproduction bedroom suites. The company was renamed, the Michigan Star Furniture Co., in 1919, and then again in 1923, as the Herman Miller Furniture Co.

Through the decades-long efforts of the DePree family and the current leadership of Michael A. Volkema, a modern, growth-oriented, financially and operationally disciplined manager, Herman Miller, a *Fortune* 1000 corporation, has become the second-largest U.S. manufacturer of office furniture.

The firm strives to create great places to work in corporate (and home) offices as well as institutional environments, such as hospitals and universities. It designs, manufactures, and sells office furniture and systems, including workstations, chairs, desks, storage cases, and file cabinets. Most of its office products are designed to be used together and interchangeably. It has consistently driven change in the office environment through design and innovation, while emphasizing community and environmental responsibility, ranking as America's third most innovative corporation, according to one *For-*

tune study, and third out of 504 corporations in another *Fortune* report on social responsibility.[1] Other experts have hailed its Eames Lounge Chair and Aeron chair as among the fifteen best-designed consumer products of the past one hundred years.[2]

The DePree Era

The DePree family, devout evangelical Christians, ran Herman Miller from 1923 to 1995. Dirk Jan (D. J.) DePree, a Baptist, joined Star Furniture as a clerk in 1909, right out of high school. He served its primary corporate leader from 1923 until 1962 and as chairman of the board from 1962 to 1969, retiring after sixty years of service to the firm. D. J.'s two sons, Hugh D. DePree and Max O. DePree, both members of the Reformed Church in America, succeeded him. Prior to Max DePree's term as chief executive officer from 1980 to 1988 and as board member until 1995, his older brother, Hugh, served as President and chief executive officer from 1962 until 1980.[3]

Max, a prominent evangelical Christian layman, served on the board of trustees at Fuller Theological Seminary for more than thirty years.[4] Founded in 1947, as a Christ-centered seminary in Pasadena, California, Fuller has engaged in modern scholarship and biblical criticism, thereby contributing to contemporary, contemplative evangelical theology.

The evangelical Christian tradition of the DePree family continues today through at least two of the firm's eleven directors, C. William Pollard, the former CEO and chairman of the board of ServiceMaster, and Thomas C. Pratt, who served as President and chief executive officer of Chuck Colson's Prison Fellowship Ministries from 1989 to 2002.[5] Four other Herman Miller directors, Mary V. Andringa, Brian Griffiths (Lord Griffiths of Fforestfach), Douglas D. French, and Ruth Alkema Reister (who retired from the board during 2003), are "well known" for their "religiosity."[6]

In 1923, D. J. DePree and his father-in-law, Herman Miller, became the majority shareholders of the Michigan Star Furniture Co. and its name changed to Herman Miller Furniture Co. in honor of DePree's father-in-law who invested some much welcomed cash.[7] During the renamed firm's early years, some of its minority shareholders were Jewish.[8] The company continued making reproductions of historic residential furniture until the 1930s.

In addition to the Great Depression ushered in by the 1929 stock market crash, the company faced a number of problems common to the furniture industry including, in D. J.'s opinion: short-lived designs; substantial discounting on closeouts; commission salesmen, some of whom represented multiple lines, who peddled what was easiest to sell; lack business identity or plan, any opportunity for repetitive manufacturing, or any contact with the product's ultimate user.[9]

The solution was forthcoming—a change to modern residential furniture—and "its arrival, D. J. believed, was providential."[10] The company turned modern design when D. J. established a reputation for excellence by contracting with celebrated furniture designers and began investing corporate funds in research and design.

The firm's modern furniture design era commenced when D. J. linked with designer Gilbert Rohde, who was Jewish.[11] D. J. described Herman Miller's turning point from selling furniture to selling a way of life as follows:

> On a hot day in July, 1930, a man came into the Grand Rapids showroom and introduced himself as Gilbert Rohde. He talked about his design philosophy. When he talked about his price, $1,000 for the design of a bedroom suite, I thought it was terrible. He had an alternate suggestion, which was three percent royalty to be paid after the furniture was sold. I figured this was a sound arrangement. How could we lose on that?
>
> Some weeks later, we received our first drawings from Gilbert Rohde. I thought they looked as if they had been done in a manual training school and told him so. 'Eye value' had become very important in selling. He replied with a letter explaining why he designed the way he did. For his designs, there should be utter simplicity: no surface enrichment, no carvings, no moldings. This brought the necessity of precision. We would not cover up with moldings and carvings. He wrote about using the best material for the job....
>
> Gilbert Rohde wrote that furniture should be anonymous. People are important, not furniture. Furniture should be useful. The room is primary. It must be planned for the people who are to live there. He was thinking about people. As a result, the furniture was space saving, utilitarian, multipurpose.[12]

Beginning in 1933, Rohde radically changed Herman Miller's design direction from handcrafted, ornate period furniture to lighter scale, twentieth-century furniture. By 1936, the firm discontinued the manufacturer of period pieces turning to high quality, modern furniture. Rhode's Executive Office Group brought the company into the office furniture market in 1942, where it had never before competed.

George Nelson, an architect, writer, and designer, who also was Jewish,[13] whom D. J. recruited in 1945, was largely responsible for creating a research- and design-driven company within all aspects of its business from manufacturing to advertising.[14] Nelson became involved in the firm's entire business operations, serving as a consultant to Herman Miller's management team. Its designers, notably Nelson, performed a vital role in the firm's business strategy, helping think through its mission, objectives, direction, and allocation of resources. According to Hugh DePree, "Herman Miller's designers [were] major participants in directing vision and resources to get results."[15] They recognized the needs and set the company's direction. For example, Nelson worked with employees responsible for translating his designs into production. He also helped with the firm's marketing.

Herman Miller built its reputation for high-end, classy, elegant furniture, based on creations from design icons, such as Charles Eames and his wife, Ray, who began their decades-long relationship with Herman Miller in 1946. The Eameses believed that design was about solving problems and producing serviceable products. Some of their solutions, like the Eames plywood chairs, introduced in 1946, using the first commercially molded and contoured plywood, became legendary. Symbolic of its innovative designs, in 1956 the company began producing the now classic Eames Lounge Chair and Ottoman. Eames provided the firm a legacy of excellence and quality.[16]

The company aggressively moved into the office market, beginning in about 1955, by entering the chair business. It was at this time that Herman Miller came to be regarded as the most innovative American office furniture manufacturer. It has, as the design leader, consistently driven innovation within the office furniture market.

Herman Miller now faced a critical business dilemma: what if the bottom fell out of its chair business? In 1958, it turned to Robert Propst, a "searcher," with a background as an artist and inventor, as well as a sculptor and teacher. His exciting, but controversial, ideas bore little or no relation to furniture. The firm formed a "research division designed to expand and intensify the company's commitment to the pursuit of diversification, to innovation, to meeting human needs, and to expanding the leadership role for Herman Miller."[17] Propst directed the research division with a view to diversification beyond the firm's furniture efforts. Raising the possibilities of new ways of looking at problems, he forced the company to see itself as a systems entity that could provide a better way of working in an office.

Propst, as an innovator, began to focus on how people should work in an office. He consulted with psychologists, anthropologists, architects, and mathematicians in a quest to enable people to work more effectively and efficiently in an office setting, while maintaining their health, interest, and job. This study enabled Propst to delineate the basic propositions subsequently incorporated in an interior system called Action Office, a system designed for people who worked in an office.[18]

In 1968, Herman Miller revolutionized the workplace by introducing Action Office II, a modular, open-plan approach to office space configuration. The product changed the firm and the industry. As the creator of the modern office environment, the company thrived in the 1970s and 1980s selling freestanding, movable partitions and modular furniture for easy reconfiguring. However, there were reductions in its international operations in the 1980s and the early 1990s.[19]

Just as growth in office furniture seemed to slow, resulting in the firm losing money in 1992,[20] the company unveiled its Aeron chair in 1994.[21] Earlier, with the launch of its Ergon chair in 1976, the firm pioneered ergonomically designed office seating. Continued research and generations of seating design led to the introduction of the groundbreaking Aeron chair, an adjustable desk chair, using a proprietary, synthetic mesh (not upholstery), designed to accommodate the ergonomic needs of any contemporary office worker, particularly those spending many hours working at a computer. Having the ability to assume the user's shape and available in multiples sizes, the Aeron chair found its place in boardrooms, offices, and homes worldwide, becoming the chair of choice among many large corporations, smaller businesses, and consumers. As a commercial success, the Aeron chair brought ergonomics to the forefront of the workplace and helped drive other ergonomically inspired designs throughout the office furniture industry. Herman Miller expanded rapidly during the mid and late 1990s, benefiting, in part, from the Internet and telecom bubble as its Aeron chair became near-synonymous with that period. The design was an enormous commercial success beginning with its introduction and today continues to dominate its category.

The Post-DePree Era

Following Richard Ruck, the first non-DePree family member who served as CEO of Herman Miller and chairman of the board's executive committee from 1988 to 1992, J. Kermit Campbell, the first externally recruited outsider, did not last long, serving as President and chief executive officer from 1992 to 1995. In May 1995, Max DePree, reaching the firm's mandatory retirement age, stepped down as chairman of the board, and Campbell was named as his successor. He had a brief reign.[22]

In the spring of 1995, Campbell began shaking things up and cutting the firm's bloated costs. In seeking to reduce its operating expenses from 30 to 25 percent of its revenues, Campbell authorized an early retirement program and the termination of about 180 employees. Distribution centers in Texas and New Jersey were closed to cut transportation costs. However, in July 1995, after the long overdue attempt to reduce corporate overhead rankled directors, a displeased board invited Campbell's resignation.

The directors then named Michael A. Volkema as the company's chief executive officer. Volkema had joined Herman Miller with its 1990 acquisition of Meridian, Inc., a maker of office filing and storage products, and came to board's notice for his strategic focus, growth-orientation, quantitative approach, and emphasis on operational reliability. The board sought (and found) in Volkema a leader who could improve morale, provide business focus, and reorganize the firm with a view to sustainable growth in sales and profits.

With Volkema's ascendancy, a younger management team took control of the firm. They looked, in part, to modern technology— the electronic frontier—to support the reinvention of Herman Miller's operations. The company's senior executives also enthusiastically embraced a new measurement tool for business performance decision-making and incentive compensation. As Volkema put it, "We say we are both serious about business and serious about people. We're also serious about technology. We are reinventing and aligning our capabilities by deploying new technologies. I don't know anyone who leads their industries who doesn't lead in the technology to support their work."[23]

The firm devised the Herman Miller Production System to improve its internal operations and customer service.[24] Beginning in 1995, it undertook a major software implementation program, under the rubric of supply chain management. It sought to overcome two traditional stumbling blocks—reliability and delivery—in the sale of furniture. The firm sought to use information technology to heighten its responsiveness to customer needs, shorten lead times, increase efficiencies, and cut inventories. These would enhance customer satisfaction as well as increase its revenues and profitability. Technology would also enable the company to strengthen its operational business model as a component assembler of finished goods.

Some of Herman Miller's technology revolution began with its SQA unit (Simple, Quick, Affordable), first launched in 1982 as Tradex, but with its new name and more advanced technologies in the early 1990s to serve small and medium-size businesses. (The name was phased-out in 2002 as part of the streamlining of the firm's numerous brands.) The SQA unit had as its top priority the speedy and reliable delivery of a slimmed-down version of the firm's existing line, with fewer choices in styles and color and fewer frills. While the cost was not necessarily less, the targeted customers received higher value, as the firm met their specific wants and needs.

To enable customers to receive their furniture accurately and on time, Herman Miller totally re-engineered its manufacturing and supply processes. It created laptop and web-based (Herman Miller's eZconnect) solutions for specification, interior design, ordering, pricing, and communication. It turned to an efficient consumer response system, based on shipping products meeting customer needs, using customer-generated information to produce and deliver customized products, thereby cutting the time to market.

New technology enabled furniture selection and layout to be processed at a client's office. Custom-designed laptop software allowed customers to select a layout on the spot with a sales representative, who used application software to configure and design office systems, cutting the design time from weeks to hours. When a customer selected a design, the software created an order list, with all the necessary parts and gave the customer a final price. Dealers and customers received a confirmation of the date of delivery within hours of order placement.

The other aspect of supply chain management focused on using internet-based technology to provide continuous and accurate material requirements so that the most reliable and efficient flow of components occurred throughout the firm's supply chain. The company deployed technology throughout its supply chain, especially in its integration with suppliers, moving to a just-in-time inventory management system. By telling suppliers what materials were needed and when, the new system enabled Herman Miller to reduce its inventories and production lead times. With supply and logistics software packages directly linking its suppliers to the company's manufacturing and assembling facilities, the firm could deliver mass, customized furniture and modular systems in two days to two weeks (versus the industry standard of six to eight weeks).[25]

Throughout the organization, Herman Miller streamlined its production processes by increasing the role of technology. It became a trailblazer on the business electronic frontier, enhancing "the reliability, speed, and efficiency of its operations."[26]

This operational model, akin to lean manufacturing, a methodology for reducing waste in specific manufacturing lines, popularized by the auto manufacturer Toyota, but broader as implemented by Herman Miller, depends on a company's relationships with reliable suppliers. The firm now uses a supplier qualification program to grade vendors on the quality and speed of their deliveries.[27] There are also capacity, financial soundness, and social responsibility components. Those who meet or outperform expectations receive more orders. Herman Miller also has a proactive supplier support program for suppliers, including training and additional resources to raise scores as well as probationary allowances. All inventory suppliers are linked electronically and have real time access as new orders are received.

Throughout the firm, the quality of its products has improved. In 1995, the company sent shipments without errors about 75 percent of the time (typical of the industry's overall performance at that time); now, error-free shipments occur more than 99 percent of the time. It also decreased the lead time it takes to build and deliver orders from eight to four weeks, with many products regularly available within ten business days after a customer places an order.[28]

Under Volkema, Herman Miller implemented the Economic Value Added (EVA) system[29] in fiscal year 1997. This system, which seeks the interests of shareholders, managers, and employees, became another key to its renaissance in the late 1990s. Properly implemented, EVA increases management's financial accountability, raises operational and financial literacy, and rewards incremental business improvement. The firm adopted EVA as a measurement tool for its overall performance and its short- and long-term business decision-making (as well as for calculating incentive compensation, discussed later) to ensure that it invests funds in those opportunities that create the highest long-term return on capital. By focusing on maximizing the company's return on capital, relative to its cost of capital, the firm looks for long-term continuous improvements in profitability and the creation of sustained economic value for its shareholders.

Together with these technological and financial innovations product design and innovation did not go unnoticed. Under Volkema, Herman Miller has continued to lead the office furniture industry in product design and innovation. In 2000, for example, the firm introduced Resolve,[30] a flexible system approach to office space utilization, based on 120-degree angles, rather than the dominant 90-degree concept. Resolve, as a way of furnishing office space, does away with the open-plan office of cubicles. It groups desks or workstations around a constellation of central maypoles, not in linear rows, using fabric screens for office definition. The wedges of workspace each feature a boomerang-shaped, adjustable desk and removable, fabric screens on each side. The 120-degree angle work system of desks, separating screens, and lighting gets rid of hard walls, replacing them with fabric screens to provide privacy.

Religious-Orientation of the DePree Family

Max DePree based his management philosophy on covenantal relationships, a concern for mutual welfare going beyond contractual relationships, traditionally based on a cash nexus. In his best-selling book, *Leadership Is an Art*,[31] DePree developed his concept of covenantal thinking. DePree stated, "Covenants bind people together and enable them to meet their corporate needs by meeting the needs of one another."[32] He continued, "Covenantal relationships fill deep needs, enable work to have meaning and be fulfilling. They make possible relationships that can manage conflict and change."[33] Ever the realist, Max realized that covenantal approaches are not easy. Rather, they are demanding to implement and maintain.

Within the context of human interactions based on covenants and the creation of mutually enabling relationships, Max saw the goals of business as twofold: first, employee development, based on the "concept of persons," which goes far beyond economic return and second, product development in terms of innovation and excellence.[34] These twin goals represented the guiding values behind the organization of Herman Miller's resources and its bringing to market distinctive, people-oriented office furniture designs.

The DePrees also had definite views on the topic of corporate leadership. They drew on the principle of biblical stewardship, introduced in Chapter 2. For Hugh DePree, "[a] leader is a steward of one's own talents, gifts, experience and knowledge. Even more, a leader is a steward of the talents and resources placed in his care."[35] He expanded on the concept of stewardship as follows, "A faithful steward recognizes the potential in those things for which he is accountable and employs them to ensure appropriate benefits for society. Thus he fulfills the call 'to love and care for one's neighbor.' As faithful stewards we achieve the primary purpose of business: to serve the user by providing products and services which improve the quality of life and culture."[36]

Max further refined the notion of stewardship. Business leaders, in his view, ought to think about their institutional heirs. They ought to leave shareholders a solid asset base, "vital financial health," and "relationships and a reputation that enable continuity of [the firm's] financial health."[37]

Influenced by Greenleaf's book, *Servant Leadership*, Max also saw the business leader as one who serves. The notion of the servant-leader, also discussed in chapter 2, rests on mutual human interdependence and accountability to God, the respect for others' welfare, and the need to take into account the more difficult, qualitative side of life. Thus, a business executive, according to Max, ought to possess a sense of responsibility for enabling others to develop, make a contribution, reach their personal and corporate potential, and have a sense of fulfillment in their work. A servant business leader strives to remove obstacles that prevent his or her employees from doing their jobs and seeks to provide greater meaning, more challenge, and more joy to employees by asking whether his or her followers are reaching their potential and whether they are learning.

Max tied the concepts stewardship and servant-leadership to his view of covenants. For him, a covenant serves as the "reference point for what caring, purposeful, committed people can be"[38] in a business entity.

Over the years, under the leadership of the DePree family, the corporation's thinking coalesced around certain principles, taking the form of a mandate, which differs from an organization's mission statement and its goals and objectives. As one management expert, who served as a consultant to Herman Miller, explained:

The mandate focuses on, and is limited to, four factors that are the total comprehensive province of management. This small number of factors belies the common opinion that management must always deal with multiple factors; it does not mean that formulating a mandate is easy. The factors are the customer...; physical resources...; financial resources; and human resources.

The word mandate implies undeniable expectations in managing these four resources. These expectations originate outside the organization, and yet they belong to every member of the organization. To educate employees about their relationship to external realities—to raise an organization's literacy—the leader's best educational tool, one that tells a credible and convincing story, is the mandate.[39]

In 1977, Herman Miller issued its mandate, after extensive work by top management, to define its business and the principles to which everyone in the company was subordinate. With financial results occupying a secondary position, the mandate provided:

Herman Miller must be an international organization in which people define and solve problems. Problem definition and problem solving—through innovation wherever possible—must result in products and services which improve the quality of life in the working and healing environments. At Herman Miller, people have the responsibility and opportunity to contribute, to participate, to be involved, to own the problem—and, indeed, to own Herman Miller.

We are committed to quality and excellence in all that we do and the way in which we do it. We seek to be socially responsible and we share a concern and responsibility for the quality of the environment in which we and our neighbors live and work.

Profit is an essential and enabling factor in all annual and long range planning and operations. Specific profit goals will be set annually. Growth is implicit but must come because of the quality of the problem solution and the potential in our people and our program.[40]

By 1986, Hugh, now retired, saw these as Herman Miller's essential values:

Excellence: In what we do and the way we do it.

Openness: The right and responsibility of all competent people to be appropriately informed so they can contribute.

Participation: The right and responsibility of people to participate, to influence and to contribute to our direction and performance through their ideas, decisions and work. It is in this value that we also assert the fundamental value of the person.

Ownership: The right of employees to own the business, to make it their own place as a result of their contributions, and also to help direct Herman Miller as participating shareholders.

Social responsibility: We expect to be a part of and a contributor to the communities in which we work and live.

The Scanlon Plan: It provides us with the best alternative we have for managing the business.

Products and services: What we make is important and it matters to us. We are dedicated to good design. We will make products and systems, along with appropriate services, that solve problems in working and living and add richness to live.

Environment: We have concern for the environment in which we work. The property and facilities we develop for our use must improve the quality of life in the communities we serve.[41]

As commissioned and edited by Volkema and the new management team in 1995-1996, with extensive, solicited input and commentary from throughout the company, domestically and internationally, the firm arrived at a statement of its five core values.[42] Herman Miller's Blueprint for Corporate Community is as follows:

Making a Meaningful Contribution to Our Customers

The mere exchange of goods and services for money is not enough for us. We have a higher aim—to make a meaningful contribution to the people we serve. We must know more about the work environment and potential solutions than anyone else. Knowledge about a customer's needs, problems, and aspirations is a necessary foundation. This knowledge alone, however, is insufficient. We want our products and services to meet customer needs, providing solutions to their problems, enabling them to reach their aspirations. Simply put, the business that understands the diverse needs of its customers, and meets those needs best, will win. We want to be that company.

Cultivating Community, Participation and People Development

We value community because of the strength and power that comes from uniting thousands of individuals, with truly diverse perspectives, opinions, skills, and backgrounds, in a common purpose. We welcome our suppliers, dealers, customers, designers, and other partners into this community. Through our diversity, united in a common purpose, we become a creative and flexible organization that adjusts rapidly to market changes.

We are a community built on competence and performance. We value community because we know that together we are more than the sum of our parts. Together we can make a contribution that we cannot make on our own. Each of us becomes something better, something richer, by participating in this community.

For 50 years, participation has been central to Herman Miller. It still is. We believe in participation because we value and benefit from the richness of ideas and opinions of thousands of people. Participation enables employee-owners to contribute their unique gifts and abilities to the corporate community. We believe that employee-owners have the obligation to contribute in their area of competence. Through participation, we serve our customers better.

Believing in the inherent worth of the people who make up this community, we realize the most important investment we make as a corporation is in developing the gifts, talents, and abilities of our employee-owners. We want them to develop new skills that will allow them to increase their contribution to the business. When we as a corporation invest in developing people, we are investing in our future. We want employee-owners to take charge of their careers, growing, building critical skills, and continuously improving. Ultimately, we believe in developing people because we are both serious about business and serious about people.

Creating Economic Value for Investors and Employee-Owners

We believe in employee ownership. We think owners make better employees. When we create value for investors, we are creating it for ourselves. The results of creating economic value are increased security, confidence, and opportunity. When our investors win, we all win. As a public company, we made a promise to our investors to create economic value. This requires us to be good stewards of our human and financial resources. Focusing on creating economic value helps us judge the value of potential investments and guides our continuous-improvement efforts....

Responding to Change Through Design and Innovation

Throughout our history..., we have met the challenge of change through design. We start with the real world, with real people, and with real problems. Design is about solving those real-world problems. Always seeking to improve and, at its best, surprise, design enables us to leap to radically new places with entirely new solutions. Design can and should be reflected in all that we do. All of us can design solutions that improve our products, our services, and our business. Great design leads to new insight, understanding and innovation. Through good design we serve our customers better than anyone else.

Living with Integrity and Respecting The Environment

We believe in doing what we say we will do, and doing what is right. We live with integrity because we believe it is the only way to do business. In a company filled with people who do what they say they will do, we can keep the promises we make to our customers, our investors, and each other.

We have a responsibility to the environment and to the communities in which we live and work. We want to reinvent the way goods are made and services are delivered, eliminating the waste and inefficiencies that degrade our environment and reduce the value we offer to customers.[43]

Non-religiously oriented firms, that is, spiritually or secularly oriented business entities, could well subscribe to these various statements of organizational values. However, Max DePree felt it important to add another element. At the end of the day and as his bottom line, he asked: "The question is not, Am I being successful? It is, Am I being faithful?" He cautioned evangelical business executives to always be on their guard, otherwise secularity would inevitably shift their thinking, noting, "[T]here is a reasonable temptation to adopt a secular standard. It happens without thinking about it. Unless somebody articulates something different, you are going to adopt a secular standard without even thinking about it."[44]

It is noteworthy, however, that the DePrees lived their religious faith but did not obligate anyone in the organization to hold those same specific beliefs, only the basic principles embodied in the firm's mandate. Yet, when asked, "Is the perception of the continuity of [the DePree] leadership sensitive to the Christian quality of the company legacy?," Max replied, "Personally, I would hope so."[45]

The DePree's Employee-Focus and the Post-DePree Era

Under Max DePree, the concept of convenantal relationships and concern with the firm's institutional value system, led to the formulation of certain principles guiding the company's practices with respect to its employees. Max's ideas had their origin with his father. D. J. had a "profound realization that working people are all extraordinary."[46] Based on this premise, he had a vision that everyone in an organization "should have the right to identity, equity, and opportunity."[47]

The ideas of the DePrees found fruition in participative management and egalitarian practices aimed at harmonizing employee-management relations as well as in efforts to promote workforce diversity.[48] Riding on the booming economy of the 1980s, Max DePree proved that corporations could be caring, nurturing places and still make lots of money. Although the 1980s were a period of overall growth, the firm was not immune to industry downturns. Reductions in its workforce occurred during this period, aggregating over five hundred people, large relative to total employment at the time, but modest compared to the early years of the twenty-first century. These actions were taken by the DePrees to reduce costs and raise profits, with the hope that a resurgence of growth would lead to renewed hiring.[49]

Even before Max and Hugh led Herman Miller, D. J. set the firm's innovative management tone by encouraging employees from different disciplines and levels to collaborate on projects and by offering widespread cash bonuses. Most notably, the company pioneered in adopting the gain-sharing Scanlon Plan.[50]

Another "providential" encounter changed the direction of Herman Miller. In October 1949, D. J. and Hugh attended a meeting sponsored by the Grand Rapids Furniture Manufacturers Association. Dr. Carl Frost, a professor at Michigan State University, spoke on the topic of "Enterprise for Everybody." Deeply affected by his thoughts on labor-management relations, D. J. and Hugh, then visited Frost at his office. On a subsequent visit to the firm's facility in Zeeland, Michigan, Frost agreed to teach the firm about the Scanlon Plan, which it adopted in 1950 and subsequently revised in 1979.[51]

To overcome the usual objection to a profit-sharing plan that the rewards are only remotely connected with workers' direct contributions, the Scanlon Plan was developed.[52] In general terms, the plan encourages employees and work groups to solve specific operational problems, thereby stimulating employees' participation in cost reduction and methods improvement. If an employee's suggestions produce lower costs or higher productivity, participation is rewarded in the form of bonuses and profit sharing. A percentage of the excess over a "normal" figure of corporate productivity is divided among all employees on a plant-wide basis, thereby promoting collaboration between management and employees and involving workers through a suggestion system and a series of committees. No one benefits individually from a suggestion.

As implemented at Herman Miller, the plan, as a group incentive arrangement based on labor productivity, covered all of its production, administrative, and service employees. The rewards of increased productivity were shared with employees through a program of monthly incentive bonuses. Under the plan, annual bonuses typically averaged slightly less than 10 percent of an employee's base wages, with an average of about 8 percent from fiscal 1990 through 1996.[53]

The DePrees were much devoted to the Scanlon Plan, both from a philosophical and a practical viewpoint. Hugh expressed the belief that the plan provided the firm with the best possible tool to manage the business with both equity and justice. For Hugh, equity was founded on the promise that everyone in an organization received the opportunity to have equal rights. These include the right to: needed, involved, informed and to understand, and to share in rewards merited by performance. Also, each person ought to have the opportunity "to own the business through personal value added" and, "at an understood time," to become a shareholder-owner, thus sharing in the risk of ownership.[54]

Max also extolled the Scanlon Plan's virtues, as a technique for practicing participative management. For him, the plan enabled "the expression of the diverse gifts of persons with an emphasis on creativity and on the quality of the process. It fuels the generation of ideas, the solving of problems, and the managing of change and conflict.... It is the constant search for what is and what can be that enables persons and groups to reach their potential."[55]

In practical terms, the DePrees saw the plan as an innovative strategy for managing an organization. It facilitated participation, with various employee committees, taking part in decision-making and assuming more responsibility for quantity, quality, and costs. It also served as an innovative compensation arrangement through a productivity sharing bonus arrangement. The firm shared the financial benefits with its employees resulting from their participation and innovation. Each person would be responsible not only for himself or herself, but for everyone in the organization. Thus, the plan enabled employees to be more responsible as well as to care and be concerned about what went on around them and throughout the organization. It taught employees how to contribute to the entity.[56]

When management of firm passed out of DePree family in 1995, Volkema, who sought a more transparent framework for incentive compensation, replaced the longstanding Scanlon Plan with the EVA system, after gaining the approval of the board of directors. The new management team regarded the entity's Scanlon Plan far less positively than the DePrees. They saw the actual metrics as changing over time. Furthermore, some metrics were viewed as subjective and not easily understood by employees (and many managers).[57]

In implementing EVA, Volkema viewed the new system as a more objective performance management and measurement system also linking the attainment of EVA improvement to incentive compensation. The new executive leadership team also promoted EVA among its employees to raise their business and financial literacy and link compensation for its executives and its workers to the interests of the firm's shareholders, including employee-owners themselves. In other words, the new system tied employees' and executives' economic interest in bonuses to a performance metric, putting powerful and widespread pressure on everyone to strive to produce good results.[58]

The firm now uses EVA to determine bonuses for its executives and rank-and-file workers, under one formula. Under prior employee and executive compensation programs, executives received a large percentage of their compensation as a bonus, based on often subjective metrics of their particular business units performance to its budget and revenue goals (subject to much annual negotiation with the better negotiators generally benefiting), while employees were compensated on the Scanlon metric. Under these old arrangements, executives "double-dipped" in that they also received individual Scanlon bonuses. With EVA, everyone works on the same objective

EVA increment target, regardless of rank, with a metric that more clearly reflects the interests of the firm's shareholders.[59]

When it developed Resolve, its new office system, coupled with other ongoing capital investments, the new management team realized that capital spending would punish the company's near-term EVA numbers and, accordingly, EVA-based incentive compensation. The firm told its workers that fiscal year 2000 would be bonus-free, thereby saving the firm $42.6 million; however, the company had earnings in a strong economy of about $140 million.[60] Many of its employees were irked because executives received incentive payouts from earlier years' performance and earned bonuses, based on a multi-year pooling system. This arrangement sought to reward performance over time by not offering quick payouts for short-term actions that might sacrifice long-term interests of employee-owners and external shareholders. However, pooled, unpaid executive bonus balances remained at risk and much of their earlier earned bonuses were lost due to negative EVA in the 2000-2002 fiscal years. Because the general plan for employees had no provision for pooling bonuses, their payouts, which averaged about 12.4 percent per year under the EVA system in fiscal years 1997-1999, were paid in full, annually.[61]

Directors and top management at Herman Miller were concerned that its employees were bearing a near-term burden for the company's significant capital investments, despite their continuing contributions to product, service, and technology advances. Some form of compensation, outside of the EVA framework, seemed appropriate. To obviate any discontent, the firm issued all of its North American-based, non-executive employees, who were with the company for the entire fiscal year, a one-time, 100 share stock option grant in June 2000, and for its international employees in February 2001.[62]

The years 2001 and 2002 proved difficult for the office furniture industry, given a sharp, significant decline in demand resulting from the unprecedented nature of capital spending cuts in both the domestic and overseas markets. With plummeting revenues and the resulting net operating loss in fiscal year 2002, EVA targets were negative and no current or past incentives were paid. In accordance with the pooling system, the few executive balances remaining from past EVA performance were eliminated, and the board determined that the EVA bonus increment would be reset for the following two fiscal years. This ensured there would be no significant payout at the expense of earnings for small, near-term increases from the low baseline figure while the company was still experiencing both negative earnings and a return on capital. As a retention and incentive tool, executives were offered opportunity to use their diminished bonus potential to purchase additional stock options, among other adjustments to executive compensation arrangements, further linking management interests to long-term corporate performance and the interests of employee-owners and external shareholders.[63]

Participative Management

Based on a belief in everyone's potential, going back to D. J., the DePrees implemented a participative management system at Herman Miller, beginning in 1950 with the adoption of the Scanlon Plan.[64] Through participation, they sought to facilitate a personal commitment by employees to business results. Participation for the DePrees connoted the opportunity for each employee to be included in the decision-making process to the level of one's competence and job responsibility. They would have a say, however, not, a vote.[65]

Max DePree's covenantal notions led him to strive to foster a business environment and work processes within which employees could develop high-quality relationships with each other, the group in which they worked, and with the firm's customers. These covenantal relationships would enable employees to get meaningfully involved in a communal endeavor.

For Max, covenantal relationships worked both ways.[66] The DePree family had a strong belief, perhaps paternalistic in its roots, going back to D. J., in the potential of people. This belief was backed up by a set of rights developed by Hugh DePree. As expanded by Max, these rights, determined by the psychological contract between management and workers, included the right to: be needed, be involved, understand, affect one's destiny, be accountable, appeal, and make a commitment.[67]

Employees shared the family's outlook toward customer service and product quality, but the firm's traditional production methods were less than efficient. Reliability only reached 75 percent (versus today's 99 percent), as rejected product parts averaged 40,000-50,000 per million versus a 2,000 per million today.[68]

Max's inclusive perspective led to his viewing all employees as insiders, which, in turn, would require extensive communication.

To keep personnel informed and involved, Max distributed some of his comments from his monthly reports, originally generated for the Scanlon work team leaders, to the firm's monthly performance review sessions so as many employees as wished to read them could.[69] Also under his leadership, Herman Miller regularly distributed videos to groups of full-time employees detailing and explaining the company's financial numbers.[70]

Today, the firm shows a video on its Monthly Business Exchange. Employees are invited to attend this forum and hear a presentation of financial numbers and a discussion of other current business issues. Sharing these financial details enables the company to continue to build the level of mutual trust and respect. The firm also communicates with its workers through a company intranet accessible to all employees.[71]

Encouraging employees to feel like part of the family was facilitated by access to senior management under the DePrees. The lowliest production worker had no difficulty knocking on Max's door. Additionally, when he was CEO, all senior vice presidents were required to meet once a month with fifteen to twenty employees over a brown bag lunch.[72]

Under Max, Herman Miller was organized around some three hundred and fifty work teams with four to twenty-five people on a team. He pondered: how could the firm maintain a sense of community and facilitate real communication when it grew to thousands of people? To try to resolve this dilemma, Max met with his six-person work team once a month over lunch with twelve to fifteen additional volunteer-employees from throughout company. Everyone brought their lunch to meetings that lasted at least one hour; no agendas were ever set. As Max recalled:

> After two or three months people found that they could trust these meetings, and they began to raise questions. They asked about this policy or that policy but never asked us to bypass supervisors to make decisions. People didn't ask to champion a personal cause or assuage a pet peeve; they readily understood the bigger picture. Pretty soon we had a waiting list for these lunches; and we found we were having direct contact with over eight hundred people a year.[73]

Today, the corporate culture remains geared to communication between executives and workers; however, because of the increased locations and number of employees, this type of contact is done by individual email or through the company intranet. Executives also meet personnel through the monthly Business Exchange events, although brown bag gatherings continue to be utilized. The company's senior management also holds employee-only annual meetings at all major facilities around the globe, reviewing the prior year, the coming year's strategy and issues, and responding to questions and concerns. Furthermore, Volkema now spends one day a year assembling products alongside workers.[74]

Even in the post-DePree era, top managers realize that when employees understand that everyone matters, they are more likely to speak their minds. According to Volkema, "Probably the first thing new employees notice here is the way people participate." He continued, "For me, employee participation is both a right and an obligation."[75] Maintaining individual employee participation, the firm asserted that it "believes that this emphasis has helped to attract and retain a capable work force."[76]

Max realized that the best people, if not the majority of those, working for corporations, even the most enlightened business entities such as Herman Miller, were similar to volunteers.[77] In times of economic prosperity, most could find other good jobs. Thus, Max maintained they needed covenants, not contracts. For him, "Covenantal relationships enable corporations...to be hospitable to the unusual person and to unusual ideas. Covenantal relationships enable participation to be practiced and inclusive groups to be formed."[78] Furthermore, covenantal relationships, according to Max, induce freedom, not paralysis. Corporations owe people "space" to grow and fulfill their potential. This sense of freedom enables employees to contribute their own unique gifts and attributes to the corporate community. Thus, he wrote, "[We] need to offer the gifts of grace and beauty to which each of us is entitled."[79]

By fulfilling deep human needs and enabling work to have meaning, Max maintained that these principles enable corporations to be hospitable not only to "unusual persons and unusual ideas," but also to "tolerate risk and forgive errors." The willingness to take risks requires accountability and the need for employees and mangers to learn together. In reflecting on his dealing with his employees, he noted, "Words such as love, warmth, personal chemistry are certainly pertinent."[80]

Yet, after Max retired in 1995, the firm's commitment to quality, covenantal relationships, based on mutual trust, frayed. Despite its professed and passionate commitment to its employees, the firm cut some 180 jobs out of 6,500 employees between May and July 1995, as part of the reorganization effort under Campbell, Volkema's predecessor. The employee-management relationship that was damaged in 1995 was generally restored by 1996.[81]

From 2001 through 2003, the firm faced the worst business environment the office furniture industry had experienced since the Great Depression. These proved to be painful years for companies in this industry, including Herman Miller, all of which fell victim to a general decline in corporate profits, the deferral of business and construction spending, the demise of technology and telecommunication firms, and a general decline in white collar employment. In response to a more than 40 percent loss in revenue and significant negative earnings in 2001 and 2002, the company began a concerted effort to become a leaner organization. Temporary manufacturing employees were eliminated in response to lower production demands. Non-essential capital and program spending were cut deeply, followed by hiring and salary freezes. Early retirement was offered to eligible employees as well as voluntary layoffs. Facilities were consolidated. Ultimately, following an exhaustive effort to pursue all other measures, in 2001 and 2002, 35 percent (3,800 people) of Herman Miller's permanent and temporary workforce was eliminated.[82] In keeping with the company's long-standing values, these employees received personal notification, substantial severance benefits, and extensive counseling (both personal and job placement). However, the firm did not reduce the salaries it paid to its directors.[83] The unprecedented economic conditions and the unavoidable actions taken in response, placed an understandable stress on employees so that some (but not all) now see Herman Miller as culturally different.

However, looking to future, under Volkema, Herman Miller wants to remain an employer of choice. The firm has formulated a "new covenant" that acknowledges that no company can promise lifetime employment with integrity, nor ever could. It continues to offer what it regards as "meaningful" participation, employee-ownership, continued learning, including a new, full tuition reimbursement plan, to sustain the broader values that have always distinguished Herman Miller.[84]

Egalitarian Approach

Max DePree implemented several egalitarian measures based, in part, on his religious beliefs. He initially addressed the compensation question after a janitor asked him what another officer was making.[85] To decrease the wage gap, he changed the firm's compensation structure limiting the CEO's cash compensation (salary and incentive bonus) directly to company's average wage. Beginning in 1984, the firm's CEO annual cash compensation could not exceed twenty times the average annual compensation of its regular, full-time workers.[86]

One time the firm's pattern shop called and said they wanted Max to meet with them. After talking about an officer's salary and why he was selling Herman Miller stock, they got into the "multiples policy." They talked about the biblical Book of Amos [Amos 2:6-7, 5:7, 11-12; 8:4-6], specifically, about God's expectation that leaders will take care of the bottom rung first, Max's "trickle-up theory."[87] He related that when they got done, one worker said:

> That makes real sense. It's so great to have you come out and explain it to us. And I'd like you to know that I really like it that I'm in my job and you're in your job.
> That's pretty great. So that's one of the ways in which we need to express a Christian standard in a secular world.[88]

However, in the post-DePree era, beginning with fiscal year 1997, Herman Miller eliminated the 20:1 cap on the CEO's cash compensation. Casting the change in terms of the implementation of its EVA Incentive Compensation Plan, the company joined in the bidding war for executive talent.[89]

It must be pointed out that the old cap was misleading in that only referenced cash compensation, including salary and incentive bonuses.[90] It did not address significant, highly rewarding, and near-invisible non-cash components only available to the most senior executives. These included: extremely generous executive defined benefit pensions in addition to the firm's general employee pension benefits which they also received; all-inclusive lifetime health care while others in the organization were subject to coverage limitations and co-payments; substantial cash-value corporate-provided life insurance policies; large stock grants and options with minimal holding requirements; corporate jet use; and significant personal expense accounts. Under the new management team, the board sold the jets, eliminated the executive-only medical coverage, the life insurance benefits, supplemental retirement arrangement, and personal expense accounts.

Second, employee stock ownership became an essential element under Max DePree, based on helping employees. When employees became shareholders, he reasoned, they would win the struggle for identity and find meaning in their work. He created an employee stock ownership plan in 1983 enabling all employees to be stockholders, thereby facilitating the firm's participatory management system. All full-time employees with more than a specified period of service could participate in the plan and buy shares at a below-market price. Under the firm's current (1995) Employee Stock Purchase Plan, in fiscal year 2003, 6,245 of its personnel were eligible to participate in the plan; of these, 1,771 (or 28 percent) were participants.[91] As of July 1999, its employees owned about sixteen percent of the firm's shares.[92]

Finding a Christian source for his business principles, independent of an economic rationale and self-interest, Max DePree stated:

> This is a chief difference in being a Christian—that you accept the idea of moving capitalism in the direction of making it possible for everyone to be a participant, to be an insider....
>
> If top management takes care of itself first, that's wrong. You are supposed to take care of the bottom of the ladder.
>
> As long as you are willing to be very open about the nonmaterialist side of life, it's not difficult [to motivate people and attract good people].[93]

Third, during the takeover wave of the 1980s, Max innovated and implemented a severance compensation (silver parachute) plan in 1986. In contrast to golden parachute approach that only protects top executives, the silver parachute plan provides severance benefits to all full-time and part-time employees (who work at least twenty hours per week) with at least two years of continuous employment with the company in case they are terminated, voluntarily or involuntarily, after a hostile takeover.[94]

Also, in fiscal year 2001 the directors authorized the chairman of the board to offer certain executives enhanced severance agreements. If within two years after a change in control, an executive terminates employment for other than for "good reason," he or she will receive a lump sum severance payment.[95]

Workforce Diversity

Max DePree emphasized that a corporate workforce must reflect God's diversity. He rested his belief on the notion that "each person is made in the image of God."[96] For Max, "The first sign of what I call God's presence is a wholehearted acceptance of human authenticity." He continued, "[W]e are God's mix—we are made in [H]is image."[97]

According to Max, "God has given people a great diversity of gifts. Understanding the diversity of our gifts enables us to begin taking the crucial step of trusting each other....God for reasons that we may not always understand, has provided us a population mix— a population mix for which leaders are held accountable."[98] For him, diversity gave others the "space to be who they are."[99] Diversity, furthermore, enabled each employee, as a unique individual, to bring his or her gifts, talents, and commitments to the group effort.[100]

Max's commitment to quality relationships based on mutual trust and his beliefs in inclusivity and God as the ultimate ethical authority led him to take strong personal action against racism.[101] Once a black woman, a friend of Max, called him at home and said they had to talk. They did so at the start of her shift the next day he realized she told him that the firm had a bigger racial problem than he realized. She called his attention to a white supervisor. Asking for her advice, she told DePree that he should personally stand up at the next monthly meeting with the firm's work team leaders and tell everyone what he believed about diversity. DePree recalling sharing his thoughts with team leaders as follows:

> I put it in the context of my faith, that we were talking about is mix. They know where I stand. The Bible tells us that we're all made in the image of God. We know we're all different, and we have to keep in mind that we're different for reasons we don't understand but God does. God makes the universe, not we....
>
> Now someone who is less secure in their faith or in their job might choose different words. But if people want to be Christian and faithful, they have to define where their faith is in these issues.[102]

DePree's faith led to his belief in diversity and his stand against racism. After DePree spoke with the team leaders, he subsequently received a hand-written note from the woman saying he had made a difference.

Today, the firm continues to believe in and practice diversity. However, Herman Miller, in one survey, ranked well, but not at the top rung, among America's one hundred best corporations in its commitment to women and minorities.[103]

Herman Miller's Environmental-Orientation

Herman Miller has long evidenced an environmental awareness. Its beliefs in environment stewardship dates back to D. J. in the 1950s.[104] Subsequently, Max DePree felt the need for the firm to use the planet's finite resources responsibly. Reflecting our interdependence and interconnectedness, he saw that no corporation could exist isolated from the needs of society and the entity's stewardship for and responsibility to succeeding generations.[105] He demonstrated the possibility for a firm to combine commercial success with caring for the environment.[106]

Environmental consciousness remains a legacy of the DePree family. Under Volkema, the company continues to rank among America's top firms in terms of its environmental responsibility.[107]

In contrast to the Pamplin Corp., it has long sought to identify "hot-button" environmental issues ahead of the curve rather than when they become large problems. Doing this gradually and proactively not reactively, is likely less expensive and less problematic in the long-run. The firm states, "We have a responsibility to the environment.... That responsibility begins with analyzing how our products are made, our services delivered, and our assets managed. When we eliminate waste that harms our environment, we act in everyone's best interest."[108] Today, the firm's environmental goal is quite simple: "To become a sustainable business—manufacturing products without reducing the capacity of the environment to provide for future generations."[109] As Volkema has noted, "Sustainability isn't just good business—it's the right thing to do."[110]

The firm evidences its seriousness about designing and implementing sustainable business practices in two key areas: waste reduction and earth-friendly materials and processes. In 1992, towards the end of the DePree family era, it created an internal working group, the Environmental Quality Action Team (EQAT), now involving over three hundred employees from all areas of the firm and striving to improve its environmental performance. This team provides direction and oversight for all its environmental activities. The EQAT sets strategies, communicates environmental objective to the firm's various stakeholders, and examines new products for their environmental impact.[111]

The company recycles or reuses nearly all the waste left over from its manufacturing processes.[112] For example, it sells fabric scraps to the auto industry to reuse as car roof linings and leather trim to luggage makers for attaché cases; stereo and auto manufacturers use vinyl for sound-deadening material. It uses returnable packaging, rugged, reusable plastic bins, rather than disposable packaging, to ship materials from its suppliers and between its factories. What cannot be recycled or reused is burned as an energy source. Its waste-to-energy plan provides a large portion of the firm's energy needs, including generating all the heating and cooling for its main building complex in Zeeland, Michigan, by burning wood waste products as fuel. The company's Energy Center, its co-generation facility, not only turns wood scraps into low cost energy, but also cuts the trash the firm hauls to landfills basically to zero.

Non-sustainable forestry practices forced a shift in the woods it uses. To protect rain forests, it eliminated tropical woods that could not be obtained from sustain-yield forest sources. Beginning in 1991, Herman Miller switched from using tropical woods, such as rosewood and seek, coming from endangered rain forests, to cherry and walnut, which do not come from the tropics. Using wood from sustainability-managed forests, the firm found that this change did not hurt its sales.[113]

Its "green" furniture is made in ways that generate less pollution and make greater use of recycled materials. The firm builds its famous Aeron chair from recycled materials with the base made from recycled aluminum and the seat shell from recycled, plastic soda bottles. The use of mesh in the chair also improves the product's environmental impact. It has also increased its use of recycled plastic, fabric, steel, or aluminum, wherever possible in its other products.[114]

The firm uses non-polluting finishes for its furniture. It switched to water-based and powder-based coating systems in place of more traditional painting or staining processes because this technology results in fewer volatile organic compounds and less environmental damage through the ease of product recycling.[115]

As a furniture assembler that farms out much of the manufacture of components, the firm evaluates its existing and potential suppliers on a number of environmental criteria under its Design for the Environment protocols. Vendors with better environmental ratings receive a larger portion of its business.[116]

In reflecting on the totality of its environmental activities, today the company notes, "[W]ith waste reduction and other environmental initiatives well under way since the early 90s, we continue to make progress toward sustainability." Many of its environmental advances followed the creation of EQAT in 1992. Under Volkema, these advances have accelerated in recent years. However, the firm has no illusions about the task ahead, stating, "Sustainability requires a long-term view: 100 percent earth-friendly processes and materials have yet to be discovered."[117]

Herman Miller's Charitable Giving

Herman Miller evidences its responsibility to the communities in which it does business. It states, "When we share a portion of our profits through our corporate giving program, we contribute to the vitality and the well-being of the communities we call home."[118]

For many years, beginning under D. J., the company made substantial, but subjective, charitable contributions. Since 1995, as formalized by its board, Herman Miller has sought to contribute 5 percent of its pre-tax income to philanthropic and community-support activities.[119] A Corporate Giving Team administers the firm's giving, with contributions over $50,000 subject to approval by the board of director's Corporate Gift Committee. The Giving Team also receives input from employees who may fill out forms to suggest donees. Volkema has also championed a more egalitarian employee committee for smaller gifts.[120]

For its employees the firm posts names of non-profit organizations needing volunteers. It encourages volunteerism through company-sponsored mentoring programs in which personnel participate during business hours as well as other volunteer endeavors, such as Habitat for Humanity projects.[121]

As revenues and profits plummeted in 2001 and 2002, accordingly, its charitable contributions markedly declined. The 2003 survey of the 100 Best Corporate Citizens placed the firm in the bottom rank of these companies for its community relations, measured in terms of philanthropy, community service projects, educational outreach, scholarships, and employee volunteerism.[122]

* * *

Ultimately, even the most progressive of firms are led back to profitability and making someone responsible for the bottom line. As Hugh DePree noted:

> Any business that is not making a profit is a poor contributor to society and a bad investment for people's money and lives. I learned this lesson from Frank Seidman [the founder of an accounting firm]. I asked him to study our business because our profits were too low, even for survival. Following a week of looking at us, he came to my office to report, "Young man, I have only one thing to tell you," he said. "Any damn fool can give it away."
>
> D. J. admits he was a poor profit producer. I saw the critical need for profit but lacked the knowledge and ability to drive for it. Vern Poest joined us and assumed the responsibility for profit. He seldom failed to ask, "Can we afford it? Can we make money on this?"[123]

But a business can be far more than making money. Under the DePree family leadership, based on the biblical principles of stewardship and servant-leadership, the firm fulfilled D. J.'s vision that a business should be "rightly judged by its humanity."[124] The question remains open whether Herman Miller will meet this test under its secular leadership in the twenty-first century.

Notes

1. Geoffry Colvin, "American's Most Admired Companies," *Fortune* 141:4, (February 21, 2000): 108-111, 7-1-F-7, at 110; Eryn Brown, "America's Most Admired Companies," *Fortune* 139:4 (March 1, 1999): 68-72, at 70.
2. Craig Vogel and Jonathan Cagan, "The 15 Best Product Designs," *Fast Company*, July 2002, available at http://www.fastcompany.com/feature/02/consumer.html.
3. Telephone Interview by author with Max DePree, January 31, 2003; Herman Miller, Inc., Archives & Records: Answers to Frequent Questions (November 28, 2001), Part 1, n.p.
4. Max DePree, *Leading Without Power: Finding Hope In Serving Community* (San Francisco, CA: Jossey-Bass, 1997), 12. Randall Balmer, *Encyclopedia of Evangelicalism* (Louisville, KY: Westminster John Knox, 2002), 231-232 and D.G. Hart, *That Old-Time Religion in America: Evangelical Protestantism in the Twentieth Century* (Chicago: Ivan R. Dee, 2002), 115-117, provide background on the Fuller Theological Seminary.
5. Herman Miller, Inc., U.S. Securities and Exchange Commission (SEC) Schedule 14A (August 29, 2002), 10-11.
6. Telephone Interview by Matthew Mantel, Reference Librarian, The Jacob Burns Law Library, The George Washington University Law School with Mark Schurman, director, External Communications, Herman Miller, Inc. (November 21, 2002).
7. Hugh DePree, *Business As Unusual: The People and Principles at Herman Miller* (Zeeland, MI: Herman Miller, 1986), 11-12; Terry Kovel and Ralph Kovel, "What About Herman Miller Bedroom Furniture?," *Dallas Morning News*, July 18, 2000, 3C.
8. DePree Interview.
9. Hugh DePree, *Business*, 14.
10. Ibid., 15.
11. DePree Interview.
12. Hugh DePree, *Business*, 15-16. Also Ibid., 41.
13. DePree Interview.
14. Herman Miller, Inc., Preliminary Prospectus (April 21, 1970), 7; Herman Miller, Inc., "Design," available at http://www. hermanmiller.com/CDA/design/0,1271, c79,00.html; Hugh DePree, *Business*, 45-47, 59.
15. Ibid., 57.
16. Ibid., 34, 47-50, 59; Jennifer Quail, "Things That Changed The World," *HFN* 76 (May 27, 2002): 58-103, at 66; James W. Blair, Jr., "Sharing a Life By Design," *Christian Science Monitor*, January 3, 2002, 15; Barbara Garet, "100 Years of Design," *Wood & Wood Products* 100:14 (January 1995): 225-273, at 263-264, 266.
17. Hugh DePree, *Business*, 83 (italics omitted).

18. Ibid., 83-84, 93-103; Garet, "100 Years," 268, 270.
19. Memorandum to author from Mark Schurman, director, External Communications, Herman Miller Inc., February 24, 2003.
20. Herman Miller, Inc., SEC Form 10-K For the Fiscal Year Ended May 28, 1994 (August 22, 1994), 10.
21. The impact of the Aeron chair is traced by Preston Lerner, "Contenders to the Throne," *Los Angeles Times Magazine*, September 29, 2002, 47; Jesus Sanchez, "The Aeron: It's Some Become the Limousine of Office Chairs," *Los Angeles Times*, April 24, 2001, Business Section C1; Beth Healy, "The Seat of Power: High-Tech Chair A Symbol of Comfort and Clout in the Workplace," *Boston Globe*, February 2, 2001, A1.
22. Justin Martin and Andrew E. Serwer, "Broken Furniture at Herman Miller," *Fortune* 132:3 (August 7, 1995): 32; Marcia Berss, "Tarnished Icon," *Forbes* 156:3 (July 31, 1995): 44-48, at 44; Susan Chandler, "An Empty Chair at Herman Miller," *Business Week* 3434 (July 24, 1995): 44-45, at 44.
23. Don Mitchell and Michael Winkleman, "Eighth Annual CE Growth 100 Index," *Chief Executive* 144 (May 1, 1999): 40-45, at 43.
24. I have drawn on *Business Week* 3699, "Rearranging the Furniture Business," (September 18, 2000): 70; Lisa H. Harrington, "A Tale of Two Planners," *Industry Week* 249:7 (April 3, 2000): 80-84, at 82, 84; Bill Roberts, "Live-Wire Supply Line," *Internet World* 5:29 (September 15, 1999): 60-63; Libby Estell, "Unchained Profits," *Sales & Marketing Management* 151:2 (February 1999): 62-67, at 64; Clint Willis, "How Winners Do It," *Forbes* 162:4 (August 24, 1998): 88-92, at 90; Frances J. Quinn, "Cutting Cycle Time and Inventory," *Logistics Management* 37:3 (March 31, 1998): 81; Doug Bartholomew, "MRP Upstaged," *Industry Week* 246:3 (February 3, 1997): 39-41, at 40-41. The growth of the SQA unit is charted by David Rocks, "Reinventing Herman Miller," *Business Week* 3625 (April 3, 2000): EB 88-96 and Bruce Upbin, "A Touch of Schizophrenia," *Forbes* 160:1 (July 7, 1997): 57-59. David Bovet and Joseph Martha, *Value Nets: Breaking the Supply Chain to Unlock Hidden Profits* (New York: John Wiley, 2000), 7-9, 169-182, provide further background on the SQA unit.
25. Ibid., 178.
26. Herman Miller, Inc., SEC Form 10-K for Fiscal Year Ended June 1, 2002 (August 26, 2002), 2.
27. Herman Miller, Inc., SEC Form 10-K/A for Fiscal Year Ended June 2, 2001 (August 21, 2001), 14.
28. Herman Miller, Inc., "Herman Miller Production System," available at http://www.hermanmiller.com/CDA/SSA/Category/ 0,1564,a4-408,00.html; Rocks, "Reinventing," at EB 98.
29. Herman Miller, SEC, Form 10-K/A for Fiscal Year Ended June 2, 2001, 11; Herman Miller, Inc., SEC Schedule 14A (August 23, 2001), 10; Herman Miller, Inc., SEC Form 10-K for Fiscal Year Ended May 29, 1999 (August 19, 1999) 10-11; Herman Miller, Inc., "Economic Value Added," available at http://www.herman miller.com/CDA/SSA/Category/0,1564,a4-c378,00.html. S. David Young and Stephen F. O'Byrne, *Eva® and Value-Based Management: A Practical Guide to Implementation* (New York: McGraw-Hill, 2001) and Gregory J. Millman, "Capital Allocation: When the Right Thing Is Hard To Do," *Financial Executive* 16:5 (September/October 2000): 28-34, at 30-31, provide a helpful introduction to EVA.
30. I have drawn on Herman Miller, SEC Form 10-K for Fiscal Year Ended June 1, 2002; Lauren Goldstein, "The Cubical Gets a Makeover," *Fortune* 142:7 (October 2, 2000): 276; Chuck Salter, "Designed to Work," *Fast Company* 33 (April 2000): 225-268.

31. Max DePree, *Leadership Is an Art* (New York: Dell, 1989). See also Stewart W. Herman, "The Potential for Building Covenants in Business Corporations," in *On Moral Business: Classical and Contemporary Resources for Ethics in Economic Life*, eds. Max L. Stackhouse, Dennis P. McCann, and Shirley J. Roels with Preston Williams (Grand Rapids, MI: William B. Eerdmans, 1995).

32. Max DePree, *Leadership Is an Art*, 15.

33. Ibid., 38.

34. Nash, *Believers in Business* (Nashville, TN: Thomas Nelson, 1994), 98-99.

35. Hugh DePree, *Business*, 146.

36. Ibid., 4.

37. Max DePree, *Leadership Is an Art*, 13.

38. Ibid., 15. Also Ibid., 12-13.

39. Carl F. Frost, *Changing Forever: The Well-Kept Secret of America's Leading Companies* (East Lansing: Michigan State University, 1996), 42 (italics omitted).

40. Hugh DePree, *Business*, 142-143 (italics omitted).

41. Ibid., 160 (italics omitted).

42. Schurman Memorandum.

43. Herman Miller, Inc., "Blueprint for Corporate Community," available at http://www2.hermanmiller.com/global/japan/en/ aboutus/etc.html; Herman Miller, Inc., 1996 Annual Report, 2-3.

44. Nash, *Believers*, 262.

45. Hugh DePree, *Business*, 178 (quoting Carl Frost).

46. Ibid., 117.

47. Ibid., 155.

48. For background on religious faith and economic values see Shirley J. Roels, "Evangelical Christians and Economic Democracy" in *On Moral Business*.

49. Schurman Memorandum.

50. Herman Miller, Preliminary Prospectus, 10.

51. Hugh DePree, *Business*, 118-123.

52. *The Scanlon Plan: A Frontier in Labor-Management Cooperation*, ed. Frederick G. Lesieur (Cambridge, MA: Cambridge Technology, 1958). See also Frost, *Changing Forever*, 7-11, 64-70, 88-96; Carl F. Frost, "The Scanlon Plan at Herman Miller, Inc.: Managing an Organization by Innovation," in *The Innovative Organization*, eds. Robert Zager and Michael P. Rosow (New York: Pergamon, 1982).

53. Hugh DePree, *Business*, 119; Schurman Memorandum; Herman Miller, Preliminary Prospectus, 10.

54. Hugh DePree, *Business,* 4-5.

55. Max DePree, *Leadership is an Art*, 88.

56. Hugh DePree, *Business*, 118-123.

57. Schurman Memorandum.

58. I have drawn on Herman Miller, Inc., SEC Schedule 14A (August 23, 2001), 10; Herman Miller, SEC Schedule 14A (August 26, 1996), 1996 Proxy Statement, 6-7; Bill Birchard, "Metrics for the Masses," *CFO* 15:5 (May 1, 1999): 64-72, at 68-69; James Bredin, "Measuring Up, Saville Row Style," *Industry Week* 247:17 (September 21, 1998): 116-117.

59. Schurman Memorandum.

60. Herman Miller, Inc., SEC Form 10-K/A, for Fiscal Year Ended June 1, 2002, 7,9; Bill Birchard and Alix Nyberg, "On Further Reflection: Do EVA and Other Value Metrics Still Offer a Good Mirror of Company Performance?" *CFO* 17:3 (March 2001): 55-64, at 64.

61. Schurman Memorandum.

62. Ibid., Herman Miller, Inc., SEC Schedule 14A (August 23, 2001), 11-12; Birchard and Nyberg, "On Further Reflection," at 64.

63. Schurman Memorandum; Herman Miller, Inc., SEC Form 10-K for Fiscal Year Ended June 1, 2002, 8, 13, 18; Herman Miller, SEC Schedule 14A (August 29, 2002), 16-18.

64. Max DePree, *Leadership Is an Art*, 24-25; Hugh DePree, *Business*, 130 (Statement of Richard Ruch, quoting Max DePree); Schurman Memorandum.

65. Max DePree, *Leadership Is an Art*, 24-25.

66. Manfred F.R. Kets de Vries, "The Dynamics of Family Controlled Firms: The Good and the Bad News," *Organizational Dynamics* 21:3 (January 1993), 59-71, at 63.

67. Max DePree, *Leadership Is an Art*, 36-42.

68. Schurman Memorandum.

69. Max DePree, *Leadership Jazz* (New York: Dell, 1992), 99-100.

70. John Case, *Open-Book Management: The Coming Business Revolution* (New York: HarperBusiness, 1995), 70; John Case, "The Open-Book Revolution" (June 1995), available at http:// www.inc.com/magazine/19950601/2296.html.

71. Schurman Interview.

72. Nash, *Believers*, 143, 150.

73. Max DePree, *Leading*, 58. See also, Max DePree, *Leadership Jazz*, 132-133.

74. Schurman Interview; Schurman Memorandum.

75. "Say What?," *Chief Executive* 146 (July 1999), 2 and 4, at 4.

76. Herman Miller, Inc., SEC Form 10-K for Fiscal Year Ended June 1, 2002, 3.

77. Max DePree, *Leadership Jazz*, 22.

78. Max DePree, *Leadership Is an Art*, 28.

79. Ibid., 17. See also Douglas J. Edwards, "The 100 Best-Managed Companies," *Industry Week* 248:15 (August 16, 1999): 44-91, at 60.

80. The quotes in this paragraph are from Max DePree, *Leadership Is an Art*, 60.

81. Schurman Memorandum.

82. Herman Miller, Inc., 2003 Annual Report, 6-8; Herman Miller, SEC Form 10-K for Fiscal Year Ended June 1, 2002, 11; Herman Miller, SEC Form 10-K for Fiscal Year Ended June 2, 2001, 16; Schurman Memorandum.

83. DePree Interview; Herman Miller, Inc., Schedule 14A (August 29, 2002), 14; Schedule 14A (August 23, 2001), 9; Schedule 14A (August 22, 2000), 14.

84. Schurman Memorandum; Telephone Interview by author with Mark Schurman, director, External Communications, Herman Miller, Inc., January 24, 2003.

85. Nash, *Believers*, 49, 149-150.

86. Herman Miller, Inc., SEC Schedule 14A (August 26, 1996), 1996 Proxy Statement, 7-8; Nash, *Believers*, 149; Peter Nulty, "The National Business Hall of Fame," *Fortune* 125:6 (March 12, 1992): 112-118, at 114.

87. Max DePree, *Leadership Jazz*, 11.

88. Nash, *Believers*, 150.

89. Herman Miller, Inc., SEC Schedule 14A (August 25, 1997), 1997 Proxy Statement, 9; Adam Bryant, "The World: Raising the Stakes: American Pay Rattles Foreign Partners," *New York Times*, January 17, 1999, Week in Review, Section 4, 1.

90. Schurman Memorandum; Herman Miller, Inc., SEC Form 10-K for Fiscal Year Ended June 1, 2002, 36; Herman Miller Inc., SEC Schedule 14A (August 22, 1995), 1995 Proxy Statement, 6.

91. Herman Miller, Inc., SEC Form 10-K for Fiscal Year Ended May 31, 2003 (August 25, 2003), 45.

92. Herman Miller, Inc., "Employee Ownership," available at http: //www.hermanmiller.com/ CDA/SSA/Category/0,1564,a1-C377,00.html.

120   Evangelical Christian Executives

93. Nash, *Believers*, 151.
94. Herman Miller, Inc., SEC Schedule 14A (August 22, 1994), 1994 Proxy Statement, 11; Kathy Bergen and Stephen Franklin, "In Era of CEO Psycho-Pay, Some Workers Still Rewarded," *Chicago Tribune*, April 30, 1997, Business Section, 2; McNulty, "Business Hall of Fame," at 114; Leonard Silk, "The Great Freedom of Corporate Life: To Question," *Business Month* 133:4 (April 13, 1989): 11-13, at 13.
95. Herman Miller, Inc., SEC Schedule 14A (August 29, 2002), 18. The Change of Control Agreement for Michael A. Volkema is set forth in Herman Miller, SEC Form 10-K for Fiscal Year Ended June 2, 2001, 64-75.
96. Max DePree, *Leadership Is an Art*, 63.
97. Max DePree, *Leading*, 180-181. See also Max DePree, *Leadership Jazz*, 57.
98. Max DePree, *Leadership Is an Art*, 63-64.
99. Nash, *Believers*, 248.
100. Max DePree, *Leadership Is an Art*, 9.
101. Nash, *Believers*, 145-146.
102. Ibid., 146.
103. *Business Ethics*, "100 Best Corporate Citizens," 17:2 (Spring 2003): 6-10, at 8.
104. Schurman Memorandum.
105. DePree, *Leadership Is an Art*, 86.
106. McNulty, "Business Hall of Fame," at 114.
107. *Business Ethics*, "100 Best Corporate Citizens," 16:2 (March/April 2002): 8-12, at 9, 12.
108. Herman Miller, Inc., "Earth Friendly, Business Savvy," available at www.hermanmiller/ CDA/category/about us/0,1243,c29,00.html. For a roadmap on how to redesign business processes to be ecologically efficient and protect the biosphere, yet still be profitable, see Paul Hawken et al., *Natural Capitalism: Creating the Next Industrial Revolution* (Boston: Little, Brown, 1999).
109. Herman Miller, Inc., "Journey to Sustainability: An Environmental Report," 3, available at http://www.hermanmiller.com/C.A./category/aboutus/0,1243,c29,00.html.
110. Herman Miller, "Earth Friendly;" Herman Miller, "Journey," 4; Mary Miller, "100 Best Corporate Citizens," *Business Ethics* 16:2 (March/April 2002): 8-12, at 9, 12.
111. Herman Miller, "Journey," 6, 11-12.
112. Eric R. Anderson, "Going Green: The Corporate Push for Environment Consciousness," *Business Credit* 94:1 (January 1992): 14-17, at 14; David Woodruff, "Herman Miller: How Green Is My Factory," *Business Week* 3231 (September 16, 1991): 54-56 at 54.
113. Herman Miller, "Journey," 10; Quail, "Things That Changed the World," at 66; Susan Caminiti, "The Payoff From a Good Reputation," *Fortune* 125:3 (February 10, 1992): 74-77, at 75.
114. Herman Miller, "Journey," 7-8; Holly Elwood and Scot Case, "Private Sector Pioneers," *Greener Management International* 29 (March 22, 2000): 70-94, at 88.
115. Herman Miller, "Journey," 9-10.
116. Ibid., 4; Elwood and Case, "Pioneers," at 91. Herman Miller asks suppliers submitting new materials for furniture to include an assessment of whether the materials meet the environmental and human health criteria of the McDonough Braungart Design Chemistry Protocol (Protocol). William McDonough and Michael Braungart, "The Anatomy of a Transformation," *Green@Work* (March/April 2002): 57-60, available at http://www. greenatworkmag.com. Working under the Protocol, in 2003 the firm introduced its new Mirra chair, relying on environmentally friendly plastics, such as a polypropylene seat back. The chair is designed to facilitate easy disassembly for recycling. Rhoda Miel, "Chair Made to Pamper People, Environment," *Plastics News* 15:22 (July 29, 2003): 22.

117. The quotes in this paragraph are from Herman Miller, "Earth Friendly."
118. Ibid.
119. Edwards, "100 Best-Managed Companies," at 60; Schurman Memorandum.
120. Ibid.; Schurman Interview.
121. Barbara B. Buchholz, "Doing Good Work," *Chicago Tribune*, December 20, 1998, Jobs Section, 1; Schurman Interview.
122. "100 Best Corporate Citizens 2003," (Spring 2003), at 8.
123. Hugh DePree, *Business*, 185.
124. Ibid., 155.

7

Interstate Batteries System of America, Inc.: From Secularism to Religion Under a Preacher-Steward Leader

Two corporations, Interstate Batteries System of America, Inc. and the R. W. Beckett Corp., similar to the two previous firms, ServiceMaster and Herman Miller, have undergone a transition. However, each of these firms has evolved from a secular-orientation to a religious-based entity. Interstate Batteries, under the leadership of a CEO who combined both preacher and steward-leadership styles, has achieved success in the replacement battery market, along with high levels of employee satisfaction and charitable giving.

Business Background

In 1952, John Searcy signed a contract with the Dallas, Texas plant of Gould National Battery under the name of Interstate Batteries System with Gould producing auto batteries for Interstate to distribute. Searcy based his start-up firm on high principles: offering the best-quality product, providing impeccable service, and treating the customer with respect.[1]

In building the company from the ground up, Searcy, as founder, and his business partner, Bill Keyes, figured out a niche in the battery arena. They set up a series of distributionships, treating their distributors with respect and dedicating themselves to their distributors' success.

From these modest beginnings, has emerged a privately owned firm with more than three hundred distributors and over two hundred thousand dealers. It provides the number one selling auto replacement battery in North America, with sales of more than 12 million units per year. It has also expanded beyond auto batteries to batteries for recreational vehicles (including boats and motorcycles) and equipment, such as telephones and toys, heavy-duty machinery, flashlights, wristwatches, fire alarms, telephones, computers, and home care. In short, it distributes, but does not manufacture, a battery to meet nearly every need. Like John Beckett at R. W. Beckett Corp., Interstate has stayed centered on its foundational business—batteries—avoiding tangents. It has focused on its core business, where it is known and where its strength lies.[2]

Recognizing the stagnant nature of the replacement car battery segment recently, it went into the retail business, setting up small, specialized retail battery stores in strip malls. At its Interstate All Battery Centers, the firm intends to provide the market with any type of battery consumers need in one spot as well as a technical department.[3]

Interstate has increased its market share through strategic promotions, designed to increase its brand awareness. Since 1992, it has sponsored the Interstate/Joe Gibbs racing team on the NASCAR circuit—the famous Interstate Batteries number 18 car. (Joe Gibbs is a National Football League Hall of Fame coach, the former coach of the Washington Redskins football team, and the owner of the Joe Gibbs NASCAR racing team.) The firm uses a duplicate of this racecar in various settings to draw crowds and promote Interstate. The firm also founded the Interstate Batteries Great American Race for pre-World War II autos which became the world's richest old car race.[4]

Today, the Interstate's annual revenues exceed $520 million. The company generally earns a net profit of one to 1.5 percent on sales, some $5 to $8 million, per year.[5]

Norman (Norm) Miller started in the battery business in 1962, when he became a traveling route driver and sales representative for his father's Interstate distributorship in Memphis, Tennessee. Offered a job by Searcy in 1964 at the firm's Dallas headquarters, Norm began traveling throughout the United States in January 1965, marketing Interstate's batteries, selling the firm's distributorships, then setting up and training the distributors.[6]

After Searcy's retirement in 1978, Norm became president and chairman of the board of Interstate. In 1991, Thomas (Tommy) Miller, his younger brother, became Interstate's president and CEO, with Norm remaining as chairman but devoting much of his time to religious activities.[7]

Norm Miller's Religious Orientation

Prior to Norm's ascendancy at Interstate in 1978, he faced a "precipitating crisis." For more than twenty years, starting at age fourteen, he had drunk to the point of blacking out, at least once a week. He needed more and more alcohol to satisfy his craving. When he went to work for Interstate, he continued to party while on the road selling batteries.

One March 1974 morning, Norm woke up with a terrible hangover. He had hit bottom. He realized he was an alcoholic who had lost control of his life. Frightened, he cried out to God, "[H]elp me! I can't handle it."[8] According to Norm, God heard and helped him. As he related, "[God] took my drinking compulsion away completely. It was instantaneous."[9]

Norm came to believe in God's power to change lives because, he felt, it was that power that turned his life around after years of drinking. Norm came to realize that there was more to life than chasing his selfish desires, his hypocrisy, hard-heartedness, bitterness, and abusive language and manner, noting, "The big payoff comes from having a personal, faithful relationship with God Himself."[10]

Later in 1974, through study, Norm accepted the claim that the Bible is "God's truth" for humanity.[11] After attending a Bible study, Norm also accepted Jesus into his life. As he recalled:

I'm not a fence-sitter, I had read the Bible enough to know that it was decision time for me.

In the Bible it says that Jesus is "the way, the truth, and the life" (John 14:6). I'd been searching for the way that would bring the truth resulting in life. I learned that we are slaves, not just to alcohol, bad habits, and other things, but overall to the S word—sin. And sin is not acceptable to God.

I knew all this was true for me, and that I had sinned against God too. But the Bible also showed me that "the truth shall make you free" (John 8:32) and Christ is the Truth! I longed for freedom. I recognized that my choices and lifestyle had indeed separated me from God, and that I could never pay God for the wrongs of my life. I read and read and finally understood the fact that Jesus had died to pay for my sins, and that I needed to humble myself before God and trust Jesus alone for forgiveness and the ability to live God's way. I understood that I could no longer avoid making a decision about Christ's claims.

So for the two hours one night after a Bible study, I sat and talked with the leader...about some of my questions. Finally, at midnight, I accepted Christ through prayer, just as the Bible teaches. I accepted Jesus into my heart as my Lord and Savior. I saw that Jesus was God's only begotten Son and that through Him we have forgiveness of sins and the power for self-control to be free—finally and for real—from the physical and emotional control of sin.[12]

Thereafter, he never doubted his decision to put his faith in Jesus. Norm read these words in the New Testament: "But the fruit of the Spirit is love, joy, peace..." (Galatians 5:22). Looking at these three words, although Scripture says more, in the weeks following his transformation, as fear left and the unconditional love came in, it affected his business behavior.[13]

For Norm, joy came from having Jesus in his heart.[14] He stated, "Words can't describe how wonderful life is in Christ!"[15] When he gave his life to Jesus, for the first time, Norm was free from the fear of business failure, thereby achieving real freedom. He stated, "It's been a wonderful freedom to be able to just try to do my best in life and not have to worry about the result of what I'm doing, and not to be driven by the compulsion of fear of failure."[16]

After receiving Jesus, he began to accept his circumstances as what was intended for him at any time. As the Apostle Paul wrote: "...[F]or I have learned to be content whatever the circumstances" (Philippians 4:11). Although making plans, setting goals, and seeking excellence, Norm accepted the results and was thankful. He received a deep inner peace which grew throughout his life.[17]

Meeting and accepting Jesus and having his existence turned upside down, Norm decided to put his faith in Jesus as well as to trust Jesus for forgiveness and the ability to live life in accordance with God's Will.[18] He came to ask himself if his thoughts and actions were pleasing to God. Deciding that all areas of his life had to square with God's way of doing things, Norm realized that he needed to make some changes. He stated, "So my approach was to go to God and His Word, to learn about what He loves and wants, and to ask Him to help me love Him more." Norm asked God to, "[H]elp [me] follow His leading in doing what He wants me to do, all the while confessing [my] sins and asking for His help."[19]

Norm was not, however, in a position to make major changes at Interstate. Although thinking about the possibilities of making his bible-based beliefs the foundation of Interstate, Norm bided his time.

When Searcy retired, Norm was then in a position to try some things in a bold, but sensitive, manner. He noted, "I prayed about how we might proclaim Christ to all our employees, and to our customers as well. I wanted everyone to experience God's great love and forgiveness."[20]

Two individuals helped Norm implement his new approach at the firm, namely, his brother Tommy, who had come to work at Interstate in 1969, and Gene Wooldridge, who joined the company in 1971. Even before Norm took control of Interstate, Norm, Tommy, and Gene shared a strong working bond, cemented by their common faith in Jesus.[21]

Implementing Norm Miller's Preacher Leadership Style

Norm sought out Tommy and Gene, inquiring about their stepping out and more forcefully sharing their belief in Jesus to their employees and customers. Norm asked them, "Can personal ministry be the bottom line in business?"[22] The three of them prayed on this. As Norm put it, God led them to start trying a few things. They decided they were going to live for and share the truth of Jesus in the firm's business. They would try to love people—Interstate employees, its distributors and dealers, and their customers—and strive to meet their needs in the context of top performance. Because Interstate would remain a closely held firm, with Johnson Controls, Inc., ultimately becoming its battery supplier and its major shareholder, it would strive to attain reasonable (but not maximum) profitability.[23]

Becoming vocal about his faith and the religious dimension of the company, Norm gradually brought God and Jesus into the workplace, when he took over the company from Searcy.[24] He asked God to help the company be "sensitive and kind, not ever desiring to offend anyone, but to be appropriately bold and obedient to share His love with others as He would lead"[25] them. Trusting Jesus more than anything, Norm sought to remold Interstate to reflect His presence.[26]

Norm developed ministry outreaches within a business context. Four expressions of his religious faith and values are notable: the firm's mission statement; its top executives looking to God for guidance through prayer; prayer and religion becoming a part of its business functions, particularly, the firm's conventions; and hiring a corporate chaplain and setting up a chaplaincy department.

First, originally drawn up in 1990-1991, the firm's current mission statement, as revised in 1998, provides:

> To glorify God as we supply our customers worldwide with top quality, value-priced batteries, related electrical power-source products, and distribution services. Further, our mission is to provide our partners and Interstate...with opportunities which are profitable, rewarding, and growth-oriented.[27]

The firm's top eight management people, including Norm, as chairman, and Tommy, as president, participated in drafting this mission statement. They met for hours weekly over several months, focusing and redefining what the firm was doing, and ultimately, coming up with the final product.[28]

Under Norm, Interstate committed its success to God. As Norm related:

> We pray and try to honor God in what we do, and His blessings are quite evident.
>
> My contention is that God's mandate to love is more important in business than just the business itself. If it seems that profits conflict with our obeying God, we try to obey God. Of course, we're not perfect by a long shot, and we often fall short. But we aim and try.
>
> I only want whatever God wants me to have. If our horizons continue to expand and we are given more opportunities to love and obey God, we will continue to give thanks and try to always honor Him and His Word. That's the only way I want to do business![29]

Second, in striving to manage Interstate's business in God's way, "lovingly, boldly, and generously,"[30] its senior executives hold regular prayer meetings, every weekday morning. At these meetings, Interstate's executive team looks to God for guidance regarding important business decisions, including hiring and firing. They ask God to direct them in how to be a witness for Him, yet be sensible in business matters. If it needs to hire someone, they ask Him to bring the firm the right people. However, if the best person is a Christian, that is fine, if not, that is also fine. The firm pursues a non-discriminatory employment policy. As Norm stated, "We obey the law; we don't hire only Christians. We try to look for the best. We pray for God to bring us the people [H]e wants and then we try to pick the best person. And if things are equal, we try to pick the most needy."[31]

Employee terminations generally present difficult problems for employers. Norm related, "We ask God to help us do the things we have to do that are best for each individual, so decisions like this [employee terminations] are the result of a consensus that's been fully covered in prayer—usually over an extended period of time." He continued, "Every day we pray about our personnel situation, asking God to help us determine if we have people in the wrong spots and, if so, where to move them. If He wants us to move people out, or bring them in, to use their gifts to the fullest in some other way, per His intentions, we want Him to make this known to us."[32]

In short, senior management committed the business to God, asking divine counsel and guidance on how to run the company, like Parker of Covenant Transport, Wade of ServiceMaster, and Beckett of the Beckett Corp., using prayer to go over business boulders and around commercial hurdles. For Norm, religion not only belongs in the workplace, it became an essential part of his life and, in turn, the firm's success. Devotion to God and Jesus, explained Norm, made Interstate the leading replacement battery manufacturer in North America. "I need to be faithful to Jesus 100 percent of the time," stated Norm, "[a]nd that includes my business."[33]

Third, prayer and religion became a part of Interstate's business functions. It opens its meetings and events with prayer, including its national conventions. However, the role of prayer goes much deeper.

As they planned Interstate's first convention, scheduled for 1984 in Hawaii, top management feared what might happen if they got all their distributors together; they were also afraid that the programs would be "lousy." Norm assembled his top management team (Tommy, Gene, and Len Ruby, who joined Interstate in 1979), telling them, "We've got to pray about this convention every day." They resorted to diligent prayer together every weekday morning for about twenty minutes, making a prayer list of everything they wanted from the convention. As Norm explained:

> First, we asked God to bathe the entire time in the love of Christ. We asked that His love would be evident even to unbelievers, that we would all be like a loving family (those were the exact words) and that there would be no dissension—none. We asked God to reveal Himself through His love and that every person involved with the convention who wasn't a believer would come to the knowledge of the Truth.[34]

As they prayed about all the details, they asked God to help them make it a successful event, in terms of everyone's safety, good weather, great meetings and presentations, and that the attendees would find the entire week to be great fun.

On Sunday morning at the first convention, not unexpectedly, the management team invited an inspirational speaker who could explain God's truth and glorify Jesus. They prayed that many, previous unbelievers, would choose to accept in Jesus.

After seeing the positive results of the first convention, with about 2,400 attendees, the firm's senior executives felt it was because they had dedicated themselves to prayer that "God had blessed and honored [their] actions."[35] Their prayers came true. At the convention, attendees told Norm, "There's something special here, a feeling of love, unity, family. These were the exact words of [their] prayers."[36]

Fourth, Norm hired the company's first chaplain and its contributions coordinator, Jim Cote, in 1987, thereby laying the foundation for the firm's chaplaincy department. Cote and Norm attended the same church. Norm knew that Cote had a good track record in his own small business; he had extensive knowledge of the Scripture; and that he, his wife and their children had an excellent reputation for trying to live their lives each day so as to honor God.

Norm brought Cote up to speed on how the executive team's commitment to operate the business in a "Christlike" manner had worked after 1978. Prior to Cote coming on board, Interstate executives and managers had prayed at all food functions with their employees and distributors, sent their distributors cards with meaningful Christian greetings at holidays, and on occasion sent them books or special messages if sickness or death occurred in a family.[37]

Cote and his successor, Henry Rogers, have implemented a pastoral ministry for the company and some of its distributors. As contributions coordinator, the chaplain also helps manage the firm's charitable giving and missionary programs. Today, Interstate's chaplaincy department offers and coordinates a number of opportunities and functions for its corporate employees, its distributors and dealers, and the wider public.[38]

Interstate employees can turn to the chaplaincy department for personal help when they have problems or suffer a loss. In addition to offering "light" counseling, the firm's chaplain, together with assistants and part-time students from the Dallas Theological Seminary, visit family members in the hospital, perform weddings, and respond to births and deaths.

Under the auspices of its chaplaincy department, the firm strives to be a witness for Jesus in the marketplace. It sponsors a corporate-wide prayer meeting on the President's National Prayer Day, which Interstate celebrates by holding a voluntary breakfast for all of its headquarters' employees. Prayer meetings are scheduled for sick employees or on other special occasions and all personnel are offered the opportunity to participate. The firm's chaplain runs a weekly, voluntary prayer group at its headquarters for executives, managers, and employees who gather to pray on various topics, such as for those who are ill.

Urgent prayer requests for its employees, their families, its distributors, and customers are put on the firm's email prayer chain and they pray for each other. Employees at its headquarters (so-called volunteer "prayees") use prayer cards provided by the chaplaincy department to pray for missionaries the firm supports. Employees can checkout Christian books, magazines, tapes and videos from its large library, supervised by the chaplaincy department. All new employees receive a Bible, a film on Jesus, and other religious information on their first day at work.

Interstate sponsors one Pizza Thursday each month for its headquarters' personnel. Bringing in Christ-centered, inspirational speakers, the firm buys pizza, with its employees inviting friends and family members to lunch. One hundred or so show up at each lunch.

Interstate also offers its employees voluntary Bible study classes, before or after work and at lunchtime. It may have three or four of these study classes going at any time.

Interstate faced a special problem—travel stress—for its national field representatives who, in calling on its distributors, are away from their families as much as twenty-one weeks a year. To give them some tools to enhance their marriages, even with the extensive travel separation, Norm and Cote developed a twelve-part video and booklet (a companion study guide), "Marriage and the Road," dealing with a dozen major issues facing its field families. This project communicates to these families how strongly the firm supports and encourages them.

Jim Cote, the firm's first chaplain was once asked about whether he encountered resentments over religion coming into the workplace. He replied:

> At first you meet some resistance, until people see that you aren't going to push them. And then you do some good and people hear about it. For instance, early on I found out about a firing. It was a case of a big person jumping on a little person and I helped get the person rehired. Word gets around.[39]

At Christmas, Interstate mails out something Christian to all its distributors and dealers. It has given away Bibles to its distributors and their employees. The firm also sends out a newsletter to its dealers that includes some references to the Bible, God, and Jesus. Sometimes the newsletter quotes Scripture or says, "If you have any interest in understanding how you can receive Jesus Christ as your Savior, contact Chaplain Henry Rogers."[40]

Like Parker of Covenant Transport, Norm has remained resolute in bringing his religious faith to the marketplace. He recalled, "We've put the message of Christ before our employees and distributors in a sensitive manner, not trying to cram anything down anyone's throats. But also we haven't stopped short because of some intimidation that maybe we shouldn't be sharing God's love."[41] Also similar to Parker, Norm maintained, "To my knowledge we haven't lost any business. We lost a couple of [dealer] accounts that were pretty good, but we sent a man in there for a week to sell and to build up the account level back up for the distribution and that eliminated the problem."[42]

In seeking to reach an even broader audience for its ministry, the firm uses its involvement in auto racing as a platform for outreach to this community and those interested in NASCAR events. For example, it distributes a pamphlet telling about NASCAR racing and an evangelical message by Joe Gibbs. It has mailed all its dealers a video of Joe Gibbs' life, his failures and successes, as a testimony to God's salvation and the goodness in Gibbs' life. Although Interstate did not get into the "racing ministry" to promote its business, the firm found that it, according to Norm, "helps the business through strengthening personal relationships."[43]

The Impact of the Firm's Leaders on Its Employees

Under Searcy, Interstate built a reputation as a fair and ethical firm. He sought to put its distributors first, to protect their interests and investments, and to take care of Interstate workers, by treating them fairly. Having an open-door policy, Searcy empowered employees holding them accountable, without constantly monitoring, correcting, or evaluating them. His people-oriented approach led to enhanced creativity and a feeling of shared responsibility throughout the organization.[44]

Under Norm, Interstate's religious orientation has impacted positively on its employees in terms of productivity and retention. According to one human resources expert, Interstate employees feel that the firm truly stands for something and cares for them. As one new employee put it, "I can't get over it, I feel I am part of a family."[45]

When asked how the company hangs onto good people so long, Norm pointed out that Interstate has this "do unto others as we would have them do unto us" mentality, which it applies to its employees. People gravitate to others who treat them well. According to Norm, when an organization treats people "with respect and look[s] after their best interests—pay[s] them well, help[s] them grow in their jobs, provide[s] good benefits, offer[s] them the prospect of a great career, encourage[s] them to feel they are on a great team—generally [it] receive[s] back in kind."[46]

The firm has also helped rehabilitate individuals who have served time in prison or who had substance abuse problems, by employing them. As Norm stated, "We have sought ways to help people work through their problems, relying on the wisdom and direction that God supplies. Some tough rehabilitation issues have been confronted along the way—we've had checks stolen and cashed, for example. But it's been worth it. Helping people is about the most enjoyable thing I've discovered in life—even if sometimes you get a bloody nose. It's the right thing to do."[47]

Norm Miller's Stewardship Exemplifies Interstate's Charitable Giving

For Norm Miller, as a steward-leader, charitable giving enables the firm to "put God's interests first...[in] the corporate world" and do "things the right way, God's way, with all the resources that ultimately [belong] to Him anyway."[48] As Jesus stated: "Do not store up for yourselves treasures on earth, where moth and rust destroy, and where thieves break in and steal. But store up for yourselves treasures in heaven, where moth and rust do not destroy, and where thieves do not break in and steal. For where your treasure is, there your heart will be also" (Matthew 6:19-21). After Norm surrendered his life to Jesus, reflecting on this passage, he sought to be a good steward when he took over management of Interstate. Corporate charitable contributions represent one expression of Norm's steward-leadership.

Thinking of charitable contributions in terms of investing, as Norm put it, Interstate gives 95 percent of its charitable funds to Christian ministries and theological education.[49] As a religion-based business, it seeks to "fund the proclamation of God's loving Word."[50] One of the major charitable ventures Interstate supports is the Dallas Theological Seminary, founded in 1924,[51] where Norm serves on the board. Today, as it has for over seventy-five years, this seminary "remains in the vanguard of the most conservative factions of evangelical theology, including no small amount of ambivalence regarding the education and public role of women."[52] However, unlike the Pamplin Corp. or Herman Miller, Interstate does not have a set percentage it seeks to give out annually to charitable groups.[53]

Serving as contributions coordinator, Interstate's chaplain manages the firm's giving program. Each charity seeking funds must complete a request form. Its chaplain and Norm, who meet every month or two, review the requests. They pray on the requests and if they want to make a contribution, then they decide on an amount.[54]

To help make a rational allocation of funds, Norm and Jim Cote (the firm's first chaplain) created a grid using the acronym, MUSIG:[55]

- M stands for multiplication and the effort to multiply the number of people who will hear the truth of Jesus and the number of people who will be trained to carry it to others;

- U stands for urgency: is it an urgent situation?

- S stands for scope: so that the broader a project's scope, generally it will be a better long-term spiritual investment.

- I stands for impact. How large a potential for impact does a venture have in terms of timing and efficiency as well as a charity's management? How much of the funds sought will go to administrative overhead? The firm wants to be able to contribute funds without any concerns because it does not attempt to control any donee, otherwise it will find another opportunity. However, its contributions are always subject to agreed upon accountability standards.

- G stands for growth. What is a venture's potential to be duplicated? Also, does it possess internal integrity, specifically, the administrative wherewithal to sustain its growth and will it fulfill its goals?

Besides its charitable contributions, the firm's employees participate in volunteer ministries it supports.[56] For instance, typically twenty or so employees go on an annual mission trip to Mexico. These mission trips give its employees exposure to projects Interstate supports. The company pays all the expenses for first-time goers, with repeat volunteers having one-half of their expenses paid by Interstate. Also, twice a year, its employees donate food and clothing to the needy at the Union Gospel Mission in Dallas. At Christmas and Easter, its personnel participate in a prison fellowship and spend time visiting inmates at a nearby jail.

*   *   *

As a preacher-steward leader, Norm Miller followed a prudent course in guiding Interstate Batteries to preeminence in its field. Offering words of sound advice for entrepreneurs and corporate executives, Norm recalled:

> We elected to grow as we desired. I'm sure Interstate Batteries could have grown a lot faster...but we agreed that just because the opportunities were there, we weren't going to forget that life's too short to be pushing ourselves into one high-risk move after another.
>
> We concluded that if any decision wasn't reasonably comfortable and within a reasonable work ethic and a sound financial risk/reward approach, we just weren't going to do it. And of course, uppermost at all times was the well-being of our distributors, their employees, the Interstate Batteries dealers, and our corporate employees.[57]

Notes

1. Norm Miller with H. K. Hosier, *Beyond the Norm* (Nashville, TN: Thomas Nelson, 1996), 59.
2. Merrill J. Oster and Mike Hamel, *The Entrepreneur's Creed: The Principles & Passions of 20 Successful Entrepreneurs* (Nashville, TN: Broadman & Holman, 2001), 71.
3. Robert Darden and P.J. Richardson, *Corporate Giants: Personal Stories of Faith and Finance* (Grand Rapids, MI: Fleming H. Revell, 2002), 240; Terry Box, "Trying to Start Something New," *Dallas Morning News*, April 13, 2002, Business Section, 1F.
4. Miller, *Beyond*, 3-10, 111-126; Richard Alm, "Closing In On the Checkered Flag," *Dallas Morning News*, November 12, 2000, Business Section, 1H.
5. Memorandum to author from Norm Miller, chairman, Interstate Batteries System of America, Inc., n.d.; Telephone Interview by Matthew Mantel, reference librarian, Jacob Burns Law Library, The George Washington University Law School with Craig Shoal, communications coordinator, Interstate Batteries System of America, Inc. (November 18, 2002); Box, "Trying to Start Something New."
6. Miller, *Beyond*, 62-63; Miller Memorandum.
7. Ibid.; Shoal Interview.
8. Miller, *Beyond*, 43.
9. Ibid.
10. Ibid., 45 (italics omitted).
11. Ibid., 44.
12. Ibid., 47-48 (italics omitted).
13. Darden and Richardson, *Giants*, 236.
14. Miller, *Beyond*, 88.
15. Ibid., 48.
16. Ibid., 130.
17. Darden and Richardson, *Giants*, 236.
18. Miller, *Beyond*, 48-49.
19. Ibid., 49.
20. Ibid., 129. See also Darden and Richardson, *Giants*, 237.
21. Miller, *Beyond*, 86.
22. Ibid., 129.
23. Ibid., 130.

24. Cheryl Hall, "A Charged Spirit," *Dallas Morning News*, April 11, 1999, Business Section, 1H.
25. Miller, *Beyond*, 130-131.
26. Ibid., 185.
27. Interstate Batteries System of America, Inc., Mission Statement available at http://www.ibsa.com/www_2001/content/ about_us/mission.asp; Shoal Interview.
28. Shoal Interview; Darden and Richardson, *Giants*, 238.
29. Miller, *Beyond*, 137-138.
30. Ibid., 152.
31. Darden and Richardson, *Giants*, 239.
32. Miller, *Beyond*, 90.
33. Dan McGraw, "The Christian Capitalists," *U.S. News & World Report* 118:10 (March 13, 1995): 52-62, at 53.
34. Miller, *Beyond*, 106 (italics omitted).
35. Ibid., 109.
36. Ibid., 106.
37. Ibid., 131.
38. Ibid., 132-137; Miller Memorandum; Shoal Interview; Telephone Interview by Matthew Mantel, reference librarian, Jacob Burns Law Library, The George Washington University Law School with Rev. Henry Rogers, corporate chaplain, Interstate Batteries System of America, Inc. (November 18, 2002); Interstate Batteries System of America, Inc., Corporate Chaplaincy available at http//:www.ibas.com/www_2001/content/about_us/ chaplaincy/chaplaincy.asp; Darden and Richardson, *Giants*, 239; Diane E. Lewis, "Workplace Spirituality Moves Up on Agenda," *Boston Globe*, December 16, 2001, G1; Gregory P. Smith, *Here Today, Here Tomorrow: Transforming Your Workforce from High-Turnover to High-Retention* (Chicago: Dearborn Trade, 2001), 67-68; Laurie Fox, "Ears to Hear," *Dallas Morning News*, May 29, 1999, Religion Section, 3G.
39. Dale Dauten, "The Good Corporate Chaplain Doesn't Let Work Get In the Way," *St. Louis Post Dispatch*, September 14, 1998, Business Plus Section, 3.
40. Darden and Richardson, *Giants*, 238.
41. Miller, *Beyond*, 131.
42. Darden and Richardson, *Giants*, 239.
43. Oster and Hamel, *Creed*, 72.
44. Miller, *Beyond*, 66, 69.
45. Smith, *Here Today*, 68.
46. Miller, *Beyond*, 90.
47. Ibid., 92.
48. Ibid., 139.
49. Ibid., 140.
50. Ibid., 145.
51. Ibid., 144, 210.
52. Randall Balmer, *Encyclopedia of Evangelicalism* (Louisville, KY: Westminster John Knox, 2002), 169.
53. Rogers Interview.
54. Ibid.
55. Miller, *Beyond*, 140-144.
56. Ibid., 132; Rogers Interview; Smith, *Here Today*, 68.
57. Miller, *Beyond*, 71.

8

R. W. Beckett Corp.: From Secularism to a Bible-Based Orientation Under a Steward-Servant Leader

The R. W. Beckett Corp. manufactures an essential but rather mundane product, burners for heating homes with fuel oil. It offers a unique perspective on a principle-based business in which faith and business coexist quite well.

With a change in top management under tragic circumstances, the Beckett Corp. evolved from a secular organization to a Jesus-centered, biblically based firm. John D. Beckett, the founder's son and longtime CEO, has combined steward and servant-leadership styles.

Business Background

John D. Beckett built his father's small business into a group of three companies. Today, these units employ nearly 600 people and generate about $100 million in annual revenues.[1]

In 1937, Reginald (Reg) W. Beckett formed a partnership with Stanton Fitzgerald under the name of the R. W. Beckett Engineering Co.[2] Working from the firm's first location, his home, Beckett began to design and build a superior oil burner for residential and commercial heating systems. Introduced at an industry trade show in 1938, the Beckett Commodore was the firm's first product. Over the years, the firm faced (and barely survived) some severe struggles.

During World War II, with fuel in tight supply and components unavailable, oil burner production came to a halt. Fuel rationing created a need to conserve energy and the company survived by shifting its focus. It turned to installing home insulation. The firm redeployed workers hired to build burners to do the insulation work.

137

Post-World War II America witnessed a surge in home construction and improvement. The company returned to its oil burner business. With homeowners switching from coal to oil heat, the firm prospered. New automatic oil heating systems provided a high level of comfort without the need to shovel coal. However, after substantial growth in the first half of the 1950s, with sales peaking at nearly 40,000 units in 1955, sales and profitability slumped, reaching critically low levels at the end of the decade. In 1960 and 1961, the company sustained losses. Faced with a changing market resulting from the widening availability and lower cost of natural gas, the company needed to revamp its product line.

While initially reluctant to redesign its respected and well-engineered products, Reg Beckett eventually launched an effort to produce a more competitive oil burner. In 1961, the company introduced the Model S (for small), a lighter, less costly oil burner, that maintained its predecessor's quality and performance. The new burner gradually revived the firm's lagging sales which in 1961 had slid to its lowest level since 1949.

In 1963, Stanton Fitzgerald, who had primary responsibility for the firm's sales and finance, told Reg of his plans to sell his one half interest and retire. When he became the sole owner, Reg asked his son, John, to join the firm, an offer John gladly accepted in December 1963. At that time, the firm had twelve employees and one million dollars of annual sales.

During 1964, Reg Beckett systematically exposed his son to every aspect of the burner business, including administration, engineering, manufacturing, marketing, and finance, providing him with priceless insight and experience. He also introduced him to the firm's suppliers and to his emerging contacts with major oil companies.

John, an eager understudy, looked forward to working together with his father for many years, as his mentor and friend, drawing on his wisdom and expertise. But that did not happen; they would only have a year together. John's dream of on-the-job mentoring was shattered when his father, who had been in apparently good health, died suddenly in February 1965, the victim of a heart attack.

On his father's death, the company was in a vulnerable position, its sales limited to just a handful of customers. The largest was a company that made furnaces for mobile homes. To John's great relief that customer took the initiative to keep Beckett as its burner supplier, risking the possibility that the company would not perform well under its new and unproven leader.

Although offers came in to buy the firm, John decided to continue the company as a Beckett family business. He recruited and began building a management team to guide the company's growth. Most notably, three months after his father's death, he hired an executive from Standard Oil of Ohio to lead the company's marketing efforts.

The organization also employed an experienced engineer to oversee its technological innovation. In 1968, it introduced Model A, a smaller, higher performance, cost-effective successor to Model S, and then Model AF (with fuel-efficient flame retention) in the early 1970s.

By the end of the 1960s, the firm's employees numbered about forty. Sales increased dramatically until the 1973 Arab oil embargo. Although the oil embargo temporarily set back the firm, the Beckett Corp. continued to penetrate new markets and expand sales. Significant sales increases occurred in the mid-1970s when homeowners replaced their old oil burners with new, more efficient units. In 1978, sales reached an all-time high, a level not surpassed until 1986. By the end of the decade of the 1970s, it employed 120 people.

The company weathered the 1979 OPEC oil shock, marked by a tripling of the price of petroleum. Although several of Beckett's competitors became discouraged, John remained confident of the industry's long-term future. In fact, Beckett personnel "hit the stump" to address influential trade gatherings with an upbeat theme: "this was a time to market actively, not retreat in desperation."

By the mid 1980s, Beckett emerged from the difficult period stronger than before. By the end of that decade, the company became the undisputed market leader. Employment increased to over 150 full-time workers.

From the late 1960s to the late 1980s, the Beckett Corp. grew at a compound growth rate in excess of 20 percent each year. Over these two decades a number of key decisions fueled the firm's growth. These included: new, talented hires in sales and engineering; focusing marketing efforts with major oil companies; forming distributor and dealer sales networks; developing new fuel-saving burner units; and expanding and improving the firm's plant and equipment. The company combined a willingness to take risks with a good customer service and a growing recognition for technological excellence.

The decade of the nineties witnessed continued corporate growth. Major themes focused on efficiency, quality products, superior manufacturing methods, and customer service. In the early 1990s, John and his management team developed and infused a set of core values into the firm, reflecting his personal religious faith. The formulation of the firm's enduring values and its Corporate Roadmap came about as part of a two-day retreat involving about twenty-five senior executives and managers of the company's three units. John presented a draft to this team, which then divided up into groups, working through various sections and making recommendations for redrafting. He then took the draft to the boards of three units for their review. Three core values, namely, integrity, excellence, and a profound respect for the individual, provided a solid foundation for the company and its future, encompassing not only the formation of its policies but also the practical aspects of relationships with its stakeholders.[3]

John then presented these core values and the Corporate Roadmap to the firm's employees, not for amending, but for their help on how to work them into the fabric of the organization. Numerous suggestions were received; some were implemented, including concerts, posters, and T-shirts.[4] Even today, the Beckett Corp. regularly communicates its three core values throughout the organization.

In the early years of the twenty-first century, the Beckett Corp. still strives to provide the best technology and innovation to the oil heating industry. It significantly improved its AFG burner, the firm's staple since the early 1980s. It also continues to develop new burner technology, including products with significantly lower emission levels.

Today, the company produces more residential oil burners than any other manufacturer in North America. To provide for management continuity within the family, in 2001, John's eldest son, Kevin A. Beckett, was named president and chief operating officer. John continues to serve as the firm's chairman and chief executive officer. But for John, "My main mission in life is to know the will of God and to do it."[5] How he got there makes for a fascinating story of his (and his firm's) unusual approach.

John Beckett's Religious Orientation

Two precipitating crises, his father's sudden death and a devastating plant fire, led John Beckett to re-evaluate his approach to his religious faith. He came to realize that difficulty is God's instrument.

Spiritual lessons must be learned. Slowly he saw that God wants to be involved in the midst of any problem, to show us the path through the difficulty and to teach us about the Divine ways.[6]

John was raised as an Episcopalian, but now attends a nondenominational, bible-based church and simply calls himself a Christian. At the core of his faith habits are daily prayer and Bible reading. The latter did not come easily.

In his early teens, his parents gave John a handsome, leather covered, black Bible with gold edged pages. After getting bogged down in genealogies and detailed rules, as perhaps many of us have, he put the Bible aside for several years, deciding it "wasn't relevant to [his] world of friends, studies, dating and sports."[7]

Years later, on the invitation of a friend, John and his wife attended a seminar at which the speaker based his teachings on biblical principles and their application to everyday living. The presenter challenged the seminar participants to read the Bible every day for at least five minutes. He accepted the challenge, but initially, reading the Bible every day took "sheer discipline."[8]

He found the New Testament more relevant. In time, his first-thing-in-the-morning Bible reading turned from a duty to a "delight," helping "nourish [his] mind and spirit throughout the day." He recalled, "Almost imperceptibly, I began looking at things differently as ideas and concepts from the Scriptures began shaping my thoughts and attitudes."[9] He now encourages business people to "think on the word, meditate on the word, and let it become alive."[10]

At his father's invitation in 1963, as noted earlier in this chapter, John joined his father's company. After his father's death in 1965, John recalled that he looked to the confidence provided by his wife and his mother, "a confidence that God was sovereign on all things, including the mystifying loss of [his] father."[11] Turning down offers to sell the company, he resolved to do all he could to make the firm succeed.

Then, a few months later in August 1965, tragedy struck again and John faced another crisis, this time an inferno. As fire engulfed its warehouse and plant, volunteer firefighters, led by John took on the battle. At the end of a long night, they were able to bring the fire under control, but the damage was horrendous. Although the fire was primarily contained in the storage area, nearly the entire burner inventory of the firm was destroyed.

In what John still sees as a "miracle" and through the efforts of devoted employee teams working around the clock and suppliers who rallied to urgent calls, the firm fulfilled each of its customer commitments on schedule.

For Beckett, keeping the business became a cause. He grew in the conviction that after his father's death and then the fire, the "business had to continue."[12] As he stated:

> For whatever reason, and whatever the company's destiny, I had been set at the helm. As painful as these experiences had been, they were producing and understanding of larger truths—truths which would be essential in achieving that destiny.
>
> An insight from that same speaker who had originally challenged me to understand more clearly how God was working in my life: "Vast areas of Scripture will never be meaningful to us unless we go through the experiences for which they give insight. It was for this reason that God allowed all of [H]is servants in Scripture to experience conflicts, and it is for this reason that we go through them as well."
>
> Dad's death, though it seemed so untimely, caused me to develop a dependence on God in ways I never would have otherwise. This upheaval probably accelerated my maturing process by years, helping me to learn to pray and to trust God more completely....
>
> The devastating fire also helped me see that we mustn't become overly secure with temporary things. I realized that factories, machinery, even customers can be here today and gone tomorrow, as can homes, bank accounts and friends. We could install sprinkler systems (and we did!), take on more insurance and exercise normal safeguards. But I was growing in the conviction that God has designed life so we can never be fully secure without [H]im.
>
> During those trying times, I found a verse in the book of Proverbs [3:5] which helped me stay properly focused. Here is what it said: "Trust in the LORD with all your heart, and lean not on your own understanding; in all your ways acknowledge Him, and He shall direct your paths." I realized that as I committed my ways more fully to God, [H]e would watch over me and over that which I held dear.[13]

John, ever the analytical engineer and now a business executive, was slow to make room for God and to enter into a more open relationship with Him. But gradually, as barriers to belief came down, he was able to conclude: "[T]he way into a full relationship with God comes through a type of death—giving up our hold on our own lives and our old way of living—and then rebirth, accepting a new life offered to us by Jesus Christ. I concluded this was what they meant by that strange phrase born again. It was not a physical thing, but a spiritual one."[14]

John made that experience his own, yielding himself to Jesus, allowing Him to be both Savior and Lord in his life. But ironically this pivotal decision prompted another.

Beckett wondered whether his involvement in business represented his true calling. Or, should he focus on a more direct type of ministry? John seriously prayed about this issue, knowing the answer would chart his vocation for years to come. Answers did not immediately follow his prayers; rather, after several months, he sensed God was asking John a key question: would he be willing to release his involvement with the family firm and follow a different path in life? After further soul-searching, John took a huge step. He turned his future and all he owned over to God. He reasoned, "This business can't be mine and yours at the same time. I don't want to hold onto this or anything else unless you want me to. If you are asking me to forego this vocation and do something different, I'm willing—willing to trust [Y]ou for the company's future and mine, whatever that may be."[15]

To his great relief, a clear answer emerged. Like Jeffrey Coors in chapter 2, John Beckett received the "unmistakable assurance" that he was where he belonged, in business, following God's call. He realized, "People called to business have many opportunities for service unavailable to those who are specifically focused on ministry vocations."[16] John pointed to the biblical Daniel, a young man taken prisoner by the Babylonians. He was a person of exceptional ability and character. His capacity to interpret dreams was so compelling that the secular king placed him in charge of a province and made him head of all the royal advisers, without compromising his faith (Book of Daniel 1:4, 6, 2:26-45, 48).

The realization that God had called John Beckett to business leadership and had placed the company in his care, led to a sense of inner peace and affirmation of God on his part, as well as a "new dimension of understanding and commitment" to his work. No longer did he doubt that he was missing "God's highest" calling for his life.[17]

Having had a strong conviction he was to run the company and do everything he could to make it succeed, led to other questions. Was it possible to apply his new dimension of faith to his work? Could he integrate a biblically based perspective into the world of business and how could that be done? From what he could see, there were no role models. But John found that God, with whom he was getting better acquainted, would guide his actions in business matters, if he would let Him.

In time John came to two basic realities: "First, there are vital aspects of your faith that can be transported into your work; and second, the Bible can serve as a dependable and unfailing guide in

making that connection." Asserting the principle of biblical inerrancy, he continued, "Over the years, I have come to a firm conviction: It is of incalculable worth to us that we have at our fingertips
the wonderful eternal truths of the Word of God." Long after each of
us is gone, "the Word of God will remain." For Beckett, the Bible
became "a reliable and practical life-directing compass." Moreover,
he noted that it "is an incredible resource to us, a sturdy and reliable
guide." Commenting on how the Bible influences his daily business
life, he concluded, "It has become for me a kind of corporate compass. The more I spend time with it, the more I am instructed, challenged, and encouraged by timeless truths that reach into every area
of my life—including day-to-day aspects of my work."[18]

John Beckett's Application of Biblical Principles to the Business World

As a biblically based firm, three key principles, a profound respect
for each employee, integrity, and the notion of sphere underpin the
Beckett Corp. This section discussed the latter two; the first principle
is considered in the section on the organization's employee focus.

Integrity serves as one of its core values, a key concept in its
mission.[19] John looks to Psalm 15 for a description of a person of
integrity, one who adheres to a standard of values. There, a person's
major character qualities are listed: he or she stands for righteous-
ness, speaks the truth from one's heart, keeps his or her word even
when it hurts, and does not accept bribes (Psalm 15:2-5).

In business, one's integrity is tested regularly. John encountered a
challenge to his integrity early in his career with a customer in Ja-
pan. The Japanese company's buying agent asked the Beckett Corp.
to pay him a "commission," in reality, a bribe, on certain sales. As
Beckett recalled, "We decided to be governed by our ethical standards and refused the payment of this 'commission,' realizing it could
cost us badly needed business. Fortunately, it didn't. The agent's
response when we refused to pay was, 'Fine. I just thought I'd ask!'"[20]

As earlier discussed, by the mid-1980s, the Beckett Corp. had
emerged as North America's largest producer of burners for residential oil heating units. It also began diversifying by starting two new
businesses in related product areas. One manufactures gas combus-
tion products; the other makes blower wheels for air moving applications. Both have become market leaders in their respective fields.

John came to the biblically based notion of "sphere"—that a business has certain areas of expertise that represent its core competencies, where it performs well. This kind of focus was neglected by ServiceMaster in its acquisition spree during the 1990s and the Pamplin Corp. For Beckett, "It's good to consider there is a larger blueprint, ordained by God, with designed spheres in which [H]e has called us to function."[21] As he stated, "It's a relief to be able to say 'no' with a clear conscience when we realize that a request is beyond our area of call or outside our sphere. This is simply the recognition that there is a blueprint for us in God's design."[22]

In arriving at the concept of sphere, Beckett drew on the Book of Acts, where we read: "From one man [H]e made every nation of men, that they should inhabit the whole earth; and he determined the times set for them and the exact places where they shall live" (Acts 17:26). For individuals, in other words, each of us was born in a particular place by God's design. He also drew on the teachings of the Apostle Paul who was conscious of God placing us into areas of responsibility when he told the Corinthians that he was determined to operate within the limits of the sphere God allotted him (2 Corinthians 10:13). By operating a business within God's appointed sphere, we remain, Beckett noted, within the boundaries of God's grace.[23]

Religious Orientation of the Beckett Corp.

Prayer became a significant factor in the business of the R. W. Beckett Corp., both in the time of crises and as an ongoing process. After his father's death, John quickly realized he could not fill all the hats his father had worn. In an effort to hire someone with marketing ability, John reached out to industry people and former college classmates. No one was willing to risk joining a small firm with an uncertain future. Having exhausted his own ideas on how to solve this problem, John turned to prayer, earnestly reaching out toward and entering into a dialogue with God with a simple, but sincere, appeal that God would send the right person to help the firm.

John's prayer was answered in an unexpected way. Bob Cook, a marketing executive of a Beckett customer, asked John to travel with him to evaluate a business opportunity. Following a successful visit, Bob inquired whether John would be open to his coming to work for the Beckett Corp. John was amazed at this apparent answer to prayer. Soon Bob joined the firm, meeting its marketing needs.[24] As John stated, "Here was God's answer to my prayer—not in the files of an executive-search firm, but comfortably seated next to me on a business trip."[25] That began a business relationship that endured for thirty-seven years, until Bob's death in 2002. As he looks back, John has no doubt that his prayer for help was wonderfully answered.

This positive resolution of a difficult situation marked the beginning of John's understanding of the importance and effectiveness of consulting with God on business matters. It built his faith in God's desire, he recalled, "for personal involvement in matters pertaining to my work."[26] Reflecting his humility and dependency he continued, "As we pray, we are acknowledging God as the source of all strength, all wisdom and insight, all grace and mercy. Through our 'dialogue' in prayer, we draw from His infinite storehouse and gain the perspective and fortitude—and yes, the faith—to function in our callings."[27]

Since the late 1960s John has met every Thursday morning with a small group of the firm's managers. At breakfast, they read Scripture and pray together. Prayer often focuses on their work, including the search for guidance on specific problems encountered and key business issues, on hiring decisions, and how to meet employee needs.

The 1979 Arab oil embargo resulted in a run-up in the price of all petroleum-based products, including heating oil. Most of the firm's major customers severely limited purchases; some stopped buying. The Beckett Corp. was vulnerable because it had just completed a major facilities expansion. In addition to cutting costs, but stopping short of laying off employees (unlike Herman Miller in recent years), Beckett employees sought Divine wisdom.

Early in 1980, twenty-five Beckett employees gathered one night after work to talk and pray together. They sought direction from God as to the company's response. As John recalled, "We affirmed our confidence that God was bigger than the Middle East crisis, and that we should take each day one at a time, with our trust in Him."[28] They came to realize that God "was showing us to...keep our focus on [H]im and watch for [H]is provision."[29] Keeping a steady course until the storm passed, the firm emerged stronger after this challenge abated.

Rather than cutting back on its product development and marketing efforts, after consultation and prayer, John decided the firm would be even more aggressive. It stepped up its product development initiatives and sent some members of its management team out on the speaking circuit, encouraging the replacement of antiquated, inefficient heating systems with modern, fuel-savings units. Increased sales enabled the firm to maintain its production levels and keep its workforce active and employed. It emerged from this traumatic time to become its industry leader, a position it has never relinquished.[30]

Similar to Covenant Transport and Interstate Batteries, prayers intersect with corporate life at Beckett in a variety of situations. If an employee makes known to John a personal difficulty, such as a health issue, John often responds, "Would you mind if I prayed for you and your situation?"[31] He has yet to have anyone decline this request.

The firm begins company events, such as dinners and special gatherings, with prayer. Groups of employees gather on a voluntary basis for Bible study and prayer. However, according to John, "[N]o pressure is ever put on folks who are not interested in participating."[32] Commenting on the significance of the voluntary Bible study and group prayers, "One of the things that's been such a blessing to us is to see how people come together," noted Penny Seaman, Beckett's director of human resources, "You can't just have faith on Sundays."[33]

The Beckett Corp.'s Employee Focus

Another precipitating crisis, this time a union organizing effort, led John to the firm's employee focus.[34] Faced with the union organizing attempt at his company, Beckett sought out a local labor attorney, known for his tough approach to labor-management disputes. Shortly into the development of a campaign to maintain a union-free environment, the attorney died suddenly.

John pondered handling the situation using his management team, rather than starting over with a new attorney. In reading from the Book of Proverbs, his eyes fell on this verse: "The way of a fool seems right to him, but a wise man listens to advice" (Proverbs 12:15). Thereafter, he located another local attorney who helped guide the campaign to rebuild employee confidence.

John wanted to preserve a direct relationship with the firm's employees, then numbering about thirty on the plant floor. He saw his genuine caring for his employees as a biblically based position.[35] He recalled Paul's letter to the church in Ephesus, where employers are reminded that the way they conduct themselves with their employees should reflect the caring and compassionate way God treats each of us (Ephesians 6:9). Thus, Beckett realized the need to do his work and bring his firm into harmony with God "in every way possible."[36]

After the employees voted to stay union-free, John came to see that he had received a wake-up call. The firm had neglected communication with its employees in a number of areas. Many aspects of its employee policies were not well understood; this led to the development of a new employee handbook. Substandard benefits were improved. Some changes in supervision were made. The firm took more seriously its growing mandate to establish closer relationships throughout the organization. As John put it, "I was now convinced we had...to work more closely together with our employees, clearly communicating our goals and aspirations and seeking the best possible work environment for every person in the company as we moved forward."[37]

Like ServiceMaster and Herman Miller under their servant-leader executives, what sets the R. W. Beckett Corp. apart from many firms is how it regards its employees. It strives to provide a supportive work environment wanting "work and work relationships to be dignified, challenging, rewarding, and enjoyable,"[38] based on the each individual's importance and worth. One of the firm's three core values to be embraced and applied throughout the organization is a "profound respect for the individual."[39] The emphasis on human dignity and the intrinsic worth of each person as well as a profound respect for the individual flows from viewing people the way God does. As John Beckett stated:

> We see that view initially in Genesis....There, in describing creation, it says God formed men and women in [H]is own image and likeness. [Genesis 1:27]. That's really quite remarkable. Attributes unique to human beings—the capacity to think, reason, worship, understand joy and sorrow, use language—all spring from God's own nature.
>
> When I saw this, it really changed the way I viewed not only myself but other people. I concluded I must place a high value on each person and never look down on another, regardless of their station or situation in life.... Since God attributes unique and infinite worth to the individual, each one deserves our profound respect.[40]

Capping the size of its business units and its pioneering maternity leave policy serve as two of the company's most notable efforts to translate the profound respect for each individual into practice. The firm tries to keep its business units to under two hundred and fifty employees, so its top executives can personally know each worker and help them in their growth and development.[41]

Through an examination of empirical studies, the firm's management team learned that the first three years of a child's life are key to forming a close mother-child bond that can produce lifelong benefits. As a result, the firm established a policy of allowing an employee the opportunity to stay home for up to twenty-six weeks, following the birth of a child. During this period, he or she receives one-quarter of his or her normal income and may borrow from the company an additional one-quarter, resulting in up to one half of normal wages. He or she may return to work part time, sharing jobs with another or working at home (either of these alternatives depends on availability), for up to three years after the birth of a child. Maternity leaves also extend to adoptive mothers.[42]

Furthermore, to emphasize the value of children, the company provides paid leave for employees traveling to adopt children as well as a $1,000 cash grant to parents for each adopted child.[43]

Respect for the individual also led the firm to offer a variety of health and educational benefits. Management and employees worked together to set up a corporate fitness center. Short courses on a variety of topics, including nutrition and personal finance, are offered during lunch breaks.

The firm's implemented two other biblically based values in its human relations practices, namely, the principle of individual gifting, echoing Max DePree of Herman Miller, and the notion of compassion. John believed, "[T]here is a direction determined by God. It is purposeful, not random. It is ordered, not disordered. Some are called in one way, others in another way. Some are gifted or equipped in a particular manner, others differently."[44] He continued, "I feel we are at our highest and best as [an] employer if we can provide a context for [each employee's] growth and enable him to find and fit in with God's blueprint for his life."[45] For Beckett, this principle is found in Paul's first letter to the Corinthians. There Paul speaks of different gifts complementing one another, using the analogy of the human body: "Now the body is not one part but of many.... But in fact God has arranged the parts in the body, everyone of them, just as [H]e wanted them to be" (1 Corinthians 12:14, 18).

The firm applies the principle of gifts in placing and promoting its employees. It seeks to give each employee the opportunity to develop his or her skills, demonstrated and latent. Recognizing that its

employees "are people of destiny," the Beckett Corp. strives to provide a "work context where nurturing, experimentation and growth
are encouraged, where God's high calling can be realized—where
they can discover and fulfill [H]is blueprint for their lives."[46]

Even as CEO, from 1965 to 1999, John interviewed every applicant to assess a willingness to work and respect authority, his or her
basic temperament, whether he or she would fit in with its employees, and most importantly whether he or she was called to work with
the firm.[47] He noted:

> I began doing it many years ago when I realized how much it built understanding and
> trust with a new employee. Of course, they're usually pretty nervous, having to meet
> the boss. But I try to put them at ease. I get them talking about themselves, their interests
> and hobbies, what they've done and what they like to do. It's amazing how valuable
> those fifteen or twenty minutes are. After all, it's the beginning of a relationship that may
> last for decades.[48]

Today John involves others, who look for the same things he would
have in the hiring process, only meeting new employees in small
groups after they join the firm.[49] In addition, the company conducts
a series of tests, seeking to match an applicant's skills with the needs
of its workplace. This includes checking references and like Interstate Batteries, the Beckett Corp. commits its hiring activities to prayer.

The firm also strives to demonstrate compassion in its work environment. Being a compassionate business enterprise is based on the
virtue as exemplified by Jesus, obviously tailored to each situation.[50]
One example: the story is well known of the woman brought to Jesus,
having been caught in the act of adultery, then punishable by ston-
ing. In response to her accusers, Jesus replied, "If any one of you is
without sin, let him be the first to throw a stone at her." One by one
the accusers left. Jesus then addressed the woman, asking if anyone
condemned her. She replied, "No one, sir." "Then," Jesus declared,
"neither do I condemn you. Go now and leave your life of sin"
(John 8:1-11).

The Beckett Corp. shows compassion to any employee who has
suffered a personal loss, such as the death of a loved one or a serious illness. Also, for those passed over for promotions, supervisors
and executives point out how they can strengthen their qualifica-
tions and encourage them to apply again for advancement. The firm
strives to be compassionate in terminating employees, cushioning
the transition with a severance arrangement and possibly the use of
an outplacement service, where appropriate. It helps a terminated

employee see the process as redemptive, one in which God can accomplish a larger purpose in the life of both of individual and the organization. As John noted, "Where it is appropriate, I would encourage the person who is being terminated to see God's hand in the process and to be in faith that if God is closing one door, [H]e's going to open another that will, in the long run, be to their benefit."[51]

In bringing the values of respect and compassion as well as the notion of gifts to the workplace, the Beckett Corp. tries to be inclusive of each employee's faith (or lack thereof). It strives to make certain that "religious beliefs have no bearing on his or her opportunity to work with or advance...; rather, we seek to view all with equal appreciation and respect."[52]

As a result of its biblically based human resource policies, the firm has become a sought after place to work. For employees beyond their first year, the firm experiences minimal turnover.[53] Reflecting on the firm's hiring practices, John concluded, "Certainly we make mistakes. But I believe that thoroughness has resulted in an exceptional workforce. Many have made the company their career, and we find a consistently high level of morale and pride. A good indication is how positively they speak about their work with friends in the community."[54]

The Beckett Corp.'s Customer Orientation

John Beckett has also emphasized the idea of customer service, based on the concept of serving, namely, putting others' interests above one's own. The Beckett Corp.'s Corporate Roadmap is a written statement of its core beliefs and values that offers direction for its entire workforce. Specifically, in regard to customers, it provides that:

> We commit to being very attentive to our customers, going beyond servicing them to satisfying their highest expectations. We pledge to be responsive, following through on commitments while avoiding any kind of arrogance or indifference. We desire to be predictable, reliable and trustworthy, willing to go the extra mile for something we believe in.[55]

Along with outstanding customer service, for instance, the tone in which telephones are answered, tactfully handling irate customers, and aggressively remedying customer problems, the firm emphasizes uncompromising product quality. Sophisticated quality control systems assure the organization backs its promises with substance. The Beckett Corp. also strives to do considerable listening, the most basic aspect of communication. As one example, the firm regularly surveys its customers and suppliers, listening for patterns or concerns which, if addressed, will strengthen the company's capabilities.

The firm also expects its internal customers to be well served. Internal transactions, which constantly occur between people in the same organization, provide another opportunity for service. Criteria for the employee-of-the month award, where employees are nominated and selected by fellow-employees, include unselfish cooperation with other personnel. Beckett supervisors are trained to serve; they coach, not boss; they facilitate, not demand; they teach, not criticize.[56]

The Beckett Corp.'s Charitable Giving

John Beckett's approach to corporate charitable giving flows from the notion of stewardship, discussed in chapter 2. Beyond its financial aspects, stewardship for him has an eternal dimension.[57] Each of us will need to give an account. The parable about the shrewd manager (Luke 16:1-12) focuses on the need for trustworthiness and faithfulness. Jesus stated: "Whoever can be trusted with very little [i.e., money] can also be trusted with much, and whoever is dishonest with very little will also be dishonest with much" (Luke 16:10).

As noted, John concluded he had a "calling" to business. More specifically, his business "needed to reflect the highest and best of what business could be." As he recalled, "It also became very clear to me that it wasn't really my business—it was God's. Instead of 'owning' it, I was set in place as a steward, watching over it as long as God desired."[58]

John sees the concept of stewardship as based on the notion that our work is God's and thus all of our resources belong to God. This notion is reflected in the organization's Corporate Roadmap as follows:

> We are not an end in ourselves but a part of God's larger purposes. As such, we are called upon to work as unto Him and to be wise and able stewards of the trust He has placed with us. We realize we are dispensable at any time in God's economy, but that it is also possible to conduct ourselves in such a way as to please Him, and find His continuing favor.[59]

A number of corporate charitable endeavors flow from the principle of stewardship, namely, giving something back and sharing with others who lack the capacity to produce. Striving to give at least 5 (and often 7 to 10) percent of the firm's after-tax profits to charity,[60] its philanthropic activities include giving the disadvantaged a start in their work careers as well as providing financial support to the worthy organizations.

During a time of high unemployment in the Cleveland area, John realized large numbers of people needed work, but were basically unemployable because of criminal records or substance abuse. In 1979, he set up Advent Industries, a significant community service activity, to provide a disciplined work environment in a supportive Christian context. Partially funded by the Beckett Corp., Advent began by doing subcontracting for the firm and other local businesses. It soon employed fifty people, most of whom were experiencing their first legitimate job. During the nearly twenty years Advent was in operation, from 1979 to 1998, twelve hundred individuals went through its demanding but supportive program, lasting six months to over two years.[61]

Advent openly encouraged Christian beliefs. The day included mandatory attendance, but not participation, at a 15-minute Bible study. Employees were paid for their attendance at this session. The only radio station allowed was a religious one. Spiritually inspiring materials were displayed in Advent's restrooms and its lunchroom.[62]

The R.W. Beckett Corp. has financially supported a wide variety of other worthy organizations, making a difference in people's lives, domestically and abroad. It sought to address systemic local problems in the areas of education and leadership development and to promote the preservation and beautification of natural resources in its community. Overseas, the corporation provided funding to dig wells in India, start micro enterprises in Africa and Central America, and fund relief efforts after flood and famine devastation. In addition to its financial support, the company has encouraged its employees to become involved in the community.[63]

* * *

As a leading, moderate sized business, the R. W. Beckett Corp. has measured up to its core values. It has achieved a reputation for integrity and excellence, rewarded with loyal customers and a high market share, some 75 to 80 percent of the North American market.[64] Furthermore, it has generated extraordinary enthusiasm among its employees, through its profound respect for each individual based on the notion that everyone is created in God's image and has demonstrated the relevance of its core values in its day-to-day activities. As Jeffrey Coors concluded, John Beckett's leadership policies and practices are "time-tested, durable and realistic."[65]

Notes

1. Telephone Interview by author with John D. Beckett, May 6, 2003.
2. I have drawn on R. W. Beckett Corp., Company History available at http://www.beckettcorp.com/companyhistory.asp; *Beckett—The First 50 Years*, available at http://www. beckettcorp.com/company; John D. Beckett, *Loving Monday: Succeeding in Business Without Selling Your Soul* (Downers Grove, IL: InterVarsity Press, 1999), 53-54.
3. Beckett Interview; R. W. Beckett Corp., Corporate Values, available at http://www.beckettcorp.com/company/corporate values.asp; John Beckett, "Noble Ideas for Business," *Management Review* 88:3 (March 1999): 62.
4. Beckett Interview.
5. *ABC World News Tonight*, September 5, 1995, Transcript #5177-7.
6. Beckett, *Loving Monday*, 105.
7. Ibid., 26.
8. Ibid., 29.
9. Ibid.; John D. Beckett, "Leadership and Legacy: One Leader's Journey in Faith," in *Faith in Leadership: How Leaders Live Out Their Faith in Their Work—and Why It Matters*, eds. Robert Banks and Kimberly Powell (San Francisco, CA: Jossey-Bass, 2000), 190.
10. Jim Braham, "The Spiritual Side," *Industry Week* 243:3 (February 1, 1999): 48-56, at 50.
11. Beckett, *Loving Monday*, 34.
12. Ibid., 39 (italics omitted).
13. Ibid., 39-40.
14. Ibid., 49-50 (italics omitted).
15. Ibid., 51.
16. Ibid., 96. See also Robert Darden and P. J. Richardson, *Corporate Giants: Personal Stories of Faith and Finance* (Grand Rapids, MI: Fleming H. Revell, 2002), 58.
17. Beckett, *Loving Monday*, 51; Beckett, "Leadership," 191-193; Dick Leggatt, "Principles and Interest," in *Profiles of Success*, eds. Ronnie Belanger and Brian Mast (North Brunswick, NJ: Bridge-Logos, 1999), 123-124.
18. The quotes in this paragraph are found in Beckett, *Loving Monday*, 78-81. See also Beckett, "Noble Ideas" and Darden and Richardson, *Giants*, 56.
19. Leggatt, "Principles," 125.
20. Beckett, *Loving Monday*, 152.
21. Beckett, "Noble Ideas."
22. Beckett, *Loving Monday*, 99.
23. Ibid.
24. Ibid., 136-137; Beckett, "Leadership," 187-188.
25. Ibid., 188
26. Ibid.
27. Ibid., 189.

28. R.W. Beckett Corp., Company History.
29. Beckett, *Loving Monday*, 138.
30. Ibid., 106-107; Beckett, "Leadership," 194-195.
31. Beckett, *Loving Monday*, 138.
32. Ibid., 139.
33. Nick Kowalczyk, "Religious Practices Establish Foothold at Certain Job Sites," *Plain Dealer* (Cleveland), August 14, 2001, C1.
34. Beckett, *Loving Monday*, 55-57; Larry Julian, *God Is My CEO: Following God's Principles In A Bottom-Line World* (Avon, MA: Adams Media, 2001), 101-102.
35. Beckett, *Loving Monday*, 56-57.
36. Ibid., 74.
37. Ibid., 57.
38. Ibid., 89.
39. R. W. Beckett Corp., Corporate Values; Beckett, Loving Monday, 89 (italics omitted).
40. Ibid., 88-89.
41. Beckett Interview.
1. 42.Ibid., 89-90.
43. Ibid., 90.
44. Ibid., 93.
45. Ibid., 95.
46. Ibid., 100.
47. Ibid., 87.
48. Ibid.
49. Beckett Interview.
50. Beckett, Loving Monday.
51. Darden and Richardson, *Giants*, 56. See also Beckett, *Loving Monday*, 112.
52. Ibid., 146-147.
53. Beckett Interview.
54. Beckett, *Loving Monday*, 88.
55. Ibid., 117–118. Jesus declared, "If someone forces you to go one mile, go with him two miles" (Matthew 5:41). Despite the added burden, it is possible to volunteer to go a second mile rather than voicing a sense of grievance at having been inconvenienced.
56. Beckett, *Loving Monday*, 118-119.
57. Ibid., 125.
58. Ibid., 123.
59. Ibid., 124.
60. Beckett Interview.
61. Beckett, *Loving Monday*, 112-113; Beckett Interview.
62. Molly Kavanaugh, "Job Training and Prayer," *Plain Dealer* (Cleveland), January 16, 1995, 1B.
63. Beckett, *Loving Monday*, 122-123.
64. Julian, *God*, 110.
65. Jeffrey H. Coors, "Foreword," to Beckett, *Loving Monday*, 10.

9

Conclusion: What Can Other Businesses Learn from These Firms and Their Executives?

The case studies in this book demonstrate that it is possible to creatively integrate competing aims, achieving positive results, both financial profitability and broader goals in line with the religious faith and values of a corporation's CEO and other top executives. As Jim Collins, the best-selling author and noted management consultant, found:

> "[M]aximizing shareholder wealth" or "profit maximization" [was not] the dominant driving force or primary objective through the history of most of the visionary companies. They have tended to pursue a cluster of objectives, of which making money is only one—and not necessarily the primary one. Indeed, for many visionary companies, business has historically been more than an economic activity, more than just a way to make money. Through the history of most of the visionary companies we saw a core ideology that transcended purely economic considerations. And—this is the key point— they have had core ideology to a greater degree than the comparison companies in our study.[1]

Thus, Collins concluded that companies that made profit maximization their top priority did not perform as well as firms that lived up to the core values of their founders often based on non-economic beliefs and the concept of an empowering culture.

A founder or a dynamic CEO may seek to implement his or her religious faith and values, as a core ideology, in an entity. However, religious beliefs, of whatever nature, can be incendiary. As a business organization grows in size, the exposition of one particular religion can lead to divisiveness among its employees and even its customers and suppliers.

In twenty-first-century America, individuals bring diverse religious (and spiritual) traditions and experiences to the office and the factory. The influx of immigrants into the United States and subsequently into the workplace has raised awareness of a vast array of the world's religions, far beyond the Judeo-Christian tradition. It is increasingly difficult to cram religious beliefs down to the throats of a firm's employees, customers, and suppliers. Additionally, the promotion of any one religious tradition in a large business entity endangers fear that it represents some sort of conspiracy to proselytize and convert everyone within the firm into thinking alike, a place where employees must be believers and share a specific religious faith to feel comfortable and be part of the team.

In any event, all but the smallest firms, in terms of number of employees, wishing to maintain a Christian identity, must comply with federal anti-discrimination laws and regulations. These provisions prohibit discrimination on the basis of religion in employment, including hiring, pay, advancement, and termination.[2] As shown by Covenant Transport, Interstate Batteries and Beckett Corp., we have seen adherence to these requirements, even in firms led by CEOs manifesting a preacher leadership style.

Leadership Through Values, Not Religious Faith

Stepping back from these concerns regarding infusing an organization with religious faith, top executives must think long and hard not only about how they want to handle the diversity of religions in the United States, but also what type of an organizational culture they are trying to build. According to one expert, "corporate culture is the pattern of shared beliefs and values that give the members of an institution meaning, and provide them with the rules for behavior in their organization."[3] Executives need to articulate a guiding business philosophy, a mission, and set of core values and organize their firm around these values. As Max DePree of Herman Miller put it, "Leaders owe a clear statement of the values of the organization. These values should be broadly understood and agreed to and should shape...corporate and individual behavior."[4]

CEOs ought to find a point of view—a big picture vision—that defines a corporation's direction—a reason why their enterprise does what it does. Because without a vision—a sense of purpose, most businesses tend to drift. A vision that is embraced can focus and galvanize an organization.

In striving to formulate a philosophy and a vision, top executives ought to consider a number of questions as they contemplate reframing of an entity's philosophy and its values and leaving an organizational legacy. Some of these include the following: What is their business about and what does it stand for? For what and to whom is their corporation responsible? Should there be a separation between the economic and the other (e.g., spiritual) aspects of a business entity? Or, can they ally their values with the running of a business and, if so, how? Can a company promote both profit and religious (or spiritual) values? Can an organization accept the whole person and allow employees to actualize their deepest aspirations? How can they put their values into practice, in the day-to-day, chaotic, working of the marketplace and the office? Can they create an organization where employees find a sense of meaning, purpose, and an acceptance of the whole person? How can an organization, its executives, and its employees embody love, compassion, and kindness in action? Specifically, how can firm relieve worker stress, deal with work-life balance questions (flexible hours, child care, and elder care), achieve gender, ethnic, religious, and racial inclusivity, among other contemporary concerns? Is a religiously (or spiritually) oriented organization compatible with competitive aggressiveness and the drive to be better than others? Can a firm's products, services, and business practices reflect values that are important to its customers? What is the firm doing for the community and for society-at-large?

To bring values into a business organization in a manner that does not cause acrimony, CEOs may be more comfortable in discussing and framing an orientation in terms of a more secular form of spirituality. Specifically, they may choose to focus on the pluralistic and ethical messages, couched in neutral language, all the world's great religions share in common, namely, integrity and truth, practicing the golden rule (goodness and service to others), love, compassion, and caring arising from the dignity of each person, the interconnectedness of all actions and beings, and the quest to plug into something large than one's self. They can use a spiritual approach to introduce values into an organization in a way few would find offensive (although some may find difficulty with any notion of a transcendent, Higher Power). In so doing, they can create an ethical, caring, inclusive firm, where community and authentic relationships exist, and make the workplace one where believers and nonbelievers can find fulfillment, yet not to divide various stakeholders, whether shareholders, employees, customers, or suppliers.

In so doing, CEOs can build on the tens of millions of spiritual seekers, perhaps totaling nearly 45 million or 24 percent of the U.S. adult population.[5] These seekers strive to grapple with big, enduring questions: What is the meaning and purpose of my life and our collective lives? Why am I and why are we here? What contributions am I and are we making? What does it all mean? Where does faith and God fit in?

These concerns with meaning and purpose and the notion that the work environment ought to be a place where employees can raise deeper questions plunge CEOs into the realm of the spirit. In the context of an increasing search for meaning and purpose in life, spirituality plays an ever-bigger role in the popular culture. The spiritual in the workplace is receiving increasing attention and is making an ever-growing impact because of the widespread interest in integrating spirituality and work.

From a hardheaded business viewpoint, senior executives want to attract, motivate, and retain creative, innovative, intrinsically motivated employees, particularly knowledge workers, who search for a workplace filled with purpose and characterized by the creation of community and meaningful relationships. Depending on how firms are run and how they treat people, these workers assess how much of their loyalty and creativity they are willing to give in return.

Placing an ever-greater importance on spiritual development, these employees yearn for meaning and fulfillment in their jobs and strive to grapple with enduring questions. They want to bring their spirits to work as well as their minds and bodies. They want to bring passion and energy to their work and find a nourishing, holistic work environment. They seek a deeper meaning, a connection to something higher. They want to find a purpose in their lives, in general, and in their work, in particular. They strive to be of service to others, see the divinity in others, and be forgiving. They do not want to compartmentalize or fragment their lives. They do not want to leave their souls at the door when they go to work. They want to be whole persons in the personal, social, professional, business, and spiritual aspects of their lives. In short, they want to live their values more fully at work.

In formulating a values-management approach, it is useful, however, to point out that some believe that there should be no expression of spirituality in a business organization. They find a focus on spirituality—whether in terms of spiritual terminology or practices—an imposition or offensive. Adherents of certain religious beliefs, especially fundamentalist, text-oriented, scriptural literalists, in particular, may object. Others may see it as another management fad to exploit or manipulate employees, for instance, by luring them into working longer hours away from their families and friends. Some may view the blurring of the line between "spirited and spiritual" as giving managers too much entrée into employees' personal lives by invading their private space—their hearts and minds. For management guru Tom Peters, "The word 'spirituality' says that you're screwing around with a part of me that I don't want touched."[6]

The Process of Organizational Change

In his book, *Leading Change*,[7] Harvard Business School Professor John P. Kotter develops an eight-step process for driving organizational change. Kotter's eight steps are as follows:

1. Establish a sense of urgency around a change initiative.

2. Create a guiding coalition to support the change initiative.

3. Develop a clear vision and strategy for driving the change.

4. Communicate the vision change thereby connecting employees to the vision and mission.

5. Empower employees for broad-based action.

6. Generate short-term wins.

7. Consolidate gains and produce more change.

8. Anchor new approaches to business and work in the organization's culture.

If a firm's top executives want to undertake a large-scale, fundamental transformation to implement a values-based orientation, whether religious, spiritual or secular, they ought to begin with Kotter's first step, establishing a sense of urgency. For example, turbulent times, such as a recession, may bring into question long-term organizational viability and success. A crisis may jolt an organization out of its comfort zone. Then, they can turn to Kotter's second step, coalition building, and his third step, re-evaluating an organization's core philosophy, goals, and values. This third step often starts with a re-examination of a firm's existing mission statement and its core values statement, if any.

A mission statement typically develops an organization's goals and the means (more specifically, the acceptable means) to attain these goals. Values focus on what the organization stands for. They define the direction of a business and its character and how employees should act in the carrying out the corporation's mission. Typically, a values statement focuses three or four items, ranked in order of importance. Thus, if a conflict arises, employees know what value(s) they should focus on.

A firm's core values may, for example, include, but are not limited to, a commitment to: first, its employees and their development, based on the mutual respect and the worth of each human being, enabling them to reach their potential through a corporate learning culture, by providing meaningful work, a more caring organization, whenever possible, and competitive wages; second, others through the production and sale of high quality products and outstanding customer service, as well as fair dealing with suppliers and customers; third, the communities in which it is located; and fourth, organizational sustainability and maximum corporate performance. Earth-conscious strategies may comprise another key value for some organizations.

These core values, which must exist within the context of competing hard in the marketplace and generating profits for its shareholders, serve as a statement of an organization's essential and enduring beliefs, the basic reasons for its existence. The mission and core values statements together guide a firm's strategy and decision-making, providing an enduring compass.

To ensure that the mission and values statements reflect the needs of the firm's people, top executives must work with and obtain input from the corporation's employees. Furthermore, these statements need to be well thought out, briefly stated in a simple, understandable manner, yet in a way that excites employees about their organization's purpose and calls forth energy and commitment. According to Max DePree, "Writing down what an institution values makes everyone come clean. It can also make people feel uncomfortable. The safety of vaguely known beliefs will disappear pretty fast."[8]

A corporate leader must take responsibility for initiating drafts of the various statements and making them understood throughout the organization. He or she ought to communicate the vision, mission, and values in a meaningful, nonthreatening way that employees can relate to and thereby reorient the entity's culture, its beliefs, ways of operating, and the behaviors that characterize human interactions within an organization. Involving all levels in shaping an entity's direction, a leader must develop a consensus among its directors, officers, managers, and employees for these statements.

By using every possible vehicle to communicate a philosophy, a mission, and a set of core values, a visionary CEO, with a compelling sense of purpose, can mobilize executives, managers, and employees for outstanding performance in fulfilling the organization's distinctive purpose and its responsibilities. This type of CEO can focus an entity's energies and guide the firm in the fulfillment of its new vision.

Ken Melrose: A Successful Visionary CEO

Kendrick B. (Ken) Melrose, chairman and CEO of The Toro Company, offers an example of how he used the biblical principle of servant-leadership to redirect a publicly held *Fortune* 1000 firm.[9] When he became CEO of Toro, then a manufacturer of lawn mowers and snow throwers, it already had achieved market leadership in these areas. Toro was, however, a traditional bottom-line organization, caring little for employee empowerment or involvement. It did not view employees as its most important asset. Rather the firm used its employees as a means to obtain the desired quantitative results: sales and production goals as well as profit targets.

When Melrose became president of Toro in 1981, everything went wrong, including an absence of snow and the onset of a recession, leading to sinking revenues and morale. In fiscal 1981, Toro lost $13 million, its first loss since 1945; it teetered on the brink of a financial crisis.[10]

After taking over, Melrose set out to change the corporate culture from a "profits first" style to a "people first" approach, based on practicing servant-leadership. He had read Greenleaf's *Servant Leadership* book, discussed in chapter 2, about leading an organization through serving, not by directing or controlling. He realized that leaders lead best by serving their employees' needs and that everyone in an organization has value and can make a meaningful contribution to the entity's success. Creating an environment for personal growth would enable people to rise to their potential. As employees achieved their potential, they would help Toro achieve its goals.

To enhance the productivity of Toro's employees and allow each to attain his or her potential, Melrose turned to a servant-leadership approach, based, in part, on his Christian faith and values. As he noted, "The Master of Men fittingly expressed the ideal of leadership in a democracy when he said, 'Whoever wants to be great among you must be your servant' [Mark 10:43; Matthew 20:26]. In my opinion, these few words from the New Testament can stand up against all the management books on the shelves today. The great leader is a great servant."[11]

Seeking to implement a servant-leader approach, Melrose sought to focus on the needs of Toro's employees, recognize its workers for their contributions, valuing relationships and through this, achieve results. As he put it, "If you take care of your employees, and eliminate obstacles and barriers to their success, then you will be in a better position to satisfy the customer. And if you satisfy the customer, you will obtain market leadership. And market leadership helps contribute to being an economically healthy and profitable company."[12]

Developing a new corporate philosophy statement, as a standard for the entity's decisions and actions, marked the first step toward changing Toro's culture, toward one based on genuinely valuing others. In communicating the need to unleash employees' potential and provide a roadmap for all its personnel to be included in the process of growing the firm, the statement provides:

> We believe the single most important factor that influences our success as a company is the Toro employee.
> Therefore, it is our privilege and responsibility to create a culture and an environment that supports and encourages individuals at Toro to achieve their highest potential.
> In order for employees to achieve that potential, we accept the responsibility to show by our actions that we care about them as individuals, understand their needs, recognize their talents, and support them in their efforts to grow and change. At the same time, all of us as employees must accept responsibility for our own performance and foster the environment that facilitates this accountability.
> As a company, and as the people of Toro, we pledge to execute this philosophy genuinely and with excellence. By doing so, we believe that Toro will be most successful in meeting its overall corporate goals.[13]

Next, Toro formulated a statement of the beliefs and values that drive its actions and decisions. Its corporate beliefs and values are as follows:

> Each individual has great potential.

That potential is best achieved when individuals are allowed to perform.

The best performance comes from those who are inspired, motivated, and encouraged; committed to the vision, goal, or task; empowered to execute the vision, and recognized for their part in completing the vision.

The leader's role is to create an environment where employees can achieve their potential as they move the company towards its goals.[14]

With the firm's philosophy established and its beliefs and values defined, Melrose then turned to the company's vision and culture. For him, vision represents "an overarching, guiding force that directs our efforts."[15] Toro's vision includes purpose, mission, and a vivid description that helps its employees to understand what the firm is trying to be and what it will be like when it gets there. Thus, for Toro:

Our Purpose is to help our customers beautify and preserve outdoor landscapes with environmentally responsible products of customer-valued quality and innovation.

Our Mission is to be the leading worldwide provider of outdoor landscaping products, support services, and integrated systems, as well as to explore new opportunities that build revenue growth and earnings sustainability using our core competencies to gain a leading market position.

Our Vivid Description paints a picture of what Toro will look like when we achieve our vision. The picture incorporates our customers' views of Toro, our products (whose innovativeness will be without precedent), and the level of our employees' contributions.[16]

Finally, Melrose focused on Toro's culture. For him, "culture tells people how to do what they do, and it determines how well they do it."[17] Over a six-month period, its management team (consisting of about seventy officers and senior managers) with input from large group meetings and small ad hoc teams of employees formulated a new culture, called Pride in Excellence.[18] Describing a culture based on mutual respect and the recognition of each employee's worth, Pride in Excellence, as it has involved, consists of two components: People Values (how employees operate and interact with one another, specifically, treating others in a valuing way) and Performance Values (what needs to happen to achieve the corporate vision, namely, excellence and goal achievement).

Toro's six People Values are: trust and respect for one another; teamwork and win-win partnerships; giving power away; coaching and serving; overtly recognizing small successes and good tries (recognition); and open, honest, clear communication.

Toro's six Performance Values are: conformance to requirements and standards; customer responsiveness; sustainable growth and profit imperatives; preventing waste by anticipating outcomes and focusing on continuous improvement (prevention); adding value through innovation and quality in product and process; and a bias for action.

In sum, the blending of the People and Performance Values embodies a culture at Toro that prizes both relationships and results. Once formulated, Pride in Excellence was communicated throughout the organization through meetings, activities and printing materials.

Implementing a Firm's New Vision, Its Mission Statement and Core Values Statement

Every change-oriented CEO needs to back up a firm's new rhetoric with his or her deep commitment. A new mission and core values must be adapted into the daily decisions and actions of a firm's employees and the entire organization. Employees must understand a firm's mission and its values and strive to implement these values daily. However, changing a corporate culture is difficult; many pitfalls abound.

A CEO must create the conditions and incentives for the new ways of thinking, deciding, working, and acting within the corporation. He or she must become the engine for organizational change.

Senior leaders must begin by embodying and implementing the firm's mission and its core values through their decisions, behavior, and actions. A corporation's top executives and those throughout the organization with enough power to lead the change must align their conduct with the firm's new direction. Demonstrating a commitment to the vision, mission, and values and incorporating them into the daily workplace, they must live the clearly defined and ordered core values through their own character and leadership, thereby serving as role models each and every day. In other words, not only must they enunciate their beliefs but they must also strive to make them an everyday reality by connecting employees to the firm's mission and its core values. Top executives must encourage others to apply the new organizational values in their decision-making and actions. They must articulate the connection between the hoped for new behavior and actions of all employees and organizational success. The incentives, structures, and practices they put in place and their own actions provide cues to an entire organization. Senior officers must demonstrate their commitment to the core values through leading by example and expending valuable resources, namely, time and money. They must strive to reinforce employees' behavior and actions and make them congruent with the firm's new direction.

A CEO needs patience and consistency. It takes time to develop a new approach, for an organization to embrace a vision, and to learn to work within a new culture.

Organizational change involves altering the knowledge, attitudes and behaviors of people throughout an entity. A need exists to change the values and norms held by an entity's members, but these deep structures are resistant to change. Beyond a CEO generating enthusiasm for a vision and new values, managers and supervisors, as well as top executives, must recognize that people have different levels of readiness in adapting to any specific change. They ought to set priorities on which changes to make in the organization, tell employees what to expect, and then let them mourn what they will have to give up.[19]

Maintaining the new environment is difficult.[20] Leaders cannot let up. Otherwise, momentum may be lost and regression may follow. They must continue to walk the talk, build trust, exercise perseverance and courage, deal with pockets of resistance, and channel the organization's energy to achieve new goals.

The selection and retention of executives, managers, supervisors, and employees is critical. The entity must choose, attract, develop and retain talented individuals who share an organization's new approach.

Ken Melrose: CEO As Successful Implementator

At Toro, Ken Melrose faced the need to implement the firm's noble philosophy, beliefs, values, vision, and culture.[21] To retrain Toro's executives and managers to serve its employees, Melrose looked to the leadership qualities of Jesus. Remembering how Jesus washed His disciples' feet, he focused his attention first on the need to demonstrate servant-leadership and then reinforce this leadership style.

He sought out visible ways to walk the talk and get the firm's top management team to buy into the new culture. Gradually, more and more of Toro's senior executives and managers not only espoused the new approach but also visibly lived it as their own. The firm assisted them in learning, practicing, and adopting the new leadership style and the requisite skills. "As an example," Melrose stated, "our officers and directors will periodically walk around the corporate offices serving coffee and donuts, or we will visit our plants and

work side-by-side with workers assembling and building components. In fact, we try to show our vulnerability by demonstrating
that we can't do the job as well as the person who owns the job."[22]

Most, but not all of the firm's executives, managers, and supervisors realigned their leadership style with Toro's people and performance values. The firm terminated those who were unable or unwilling to do so.

The servant-leadership model filtered down through the various
levels at Toro. As Melrose explained, "I try to demonstrate leadership in a way that models the expected behaviors so that other leaders are encouraged to do the same thing with their staff, and this
cascades throughout the organizational structure. What you end up
with is managers not trying to direct and control their people, but try
to coach and serve their people to be motivated and empowered,
and to get better and better in what they do."[23]

To reinforce the servant-leadership approach, Toro developed a
new performance appraisal system and attached financial consequences to the rankings. Part of the annual incentive compensation
for its senior executives and managers reflects how successfully they
have practiced the new Toro culture, as judged by their peers and
subordinates. These performance reviews assess, in part, those areas where a manager's behavior inhibits employees from quality
work or obtaining their goals, or is otherwise inconsistent with Toro's
employee-oriented philosophy.[24]

Over the years, Toro has evolved from a manufacturer of lawn
mowers and snow throwers to become a worldwide provider of products, services, and systems for the preservation and enhancement of
the outdoor environment. Bottom-line results followed at Toro from
its people-oriented approach. Sales and earnings have consistently
grown as has shareholder value. Its sales per employee and its product innovation lead the industry. Its annual employee turnover rate
(about 5.4 percent) is substantially less than the consumer durable
goods industry rate of 7 to 8 percent.

Difficult economic times force hard choices. Will executives resist the easy choices to achieve short-term cost savings, for example,
through ceasing to hire, laying off employees (or forcing them to
work reduced hours), curtailing training, freezing or cutting pay,
holding up promotions, or using temporary help?[26] Or, will a firm
continue to focus on "people-based strategies,"[27] including building
the skills and competencies of its employees?

A Toro plant in Shakopee, Minnesota, provides an example of the latter approach. Faced with seasonal business swings, management contemplated laying off employees at that facility. At the same time, however, the company had a problem with one of its products in the field. Devising a redeployment strategy, managers decided to move the plant's employees temporarily into the field to help its distributors solve the problem. Going out into parks and golf courses, these employees, who continued to work, received a valuable learning experience. Toro customers were happy with the one-on-one service they received.[28]

* * *

Organizational transformation, particularly the formulation and implementation of a new corporate governance model, requires a tremendous commitment, as well as patience and persistence, from a firm's senior executives to build and sustain such an environment. What is required is pragmatic, but idealistic, leaders with their own sense of meaning and purpose who can build and sustain authentic relationships, thereby, facilitating the actualization of others, helping them grow and develop, personally and professionally. Based on the need to develop their respect for others and the personal growth for all, they ought to encourage team-building, synergy, and win-win thinking within the organization as well as with its customers and suppliers. These value-oriented leaders will also build flexible, sustainable, and competitive corporations, providing long-term earnings growth, thereby satisfying the financial requirements of shareholders and investors. They will create business organizations meeting ownership and other stakeholder needs.

Notes

1. James C. Collins and Jerry I. Porras, *Built to Last: Successful Habits of Visionary Companies* (New York: HarperBusiness, 1994), 55 (italics omitted).
2. Title VII of the Civil Rights Act of 1964 prohibits discrimination on the basis of religion, among other grounds, by private employees "engaged in an industry affecting commerce who has fifteen or more employees for each working day in each of twenty or more calendar weeks in the current or proceeding calendar year...." 42 USC § 2000e(b), (e)-2(a) and (m).
3. Stanley M. Davis, *Managing Corporate Culture* (Cambridge, MA: Ballinger, 1984), n 1, at 1.
4. Max DePree, *Leadership Is an Art* (New York: Dell, 1989), 14.
5. Paul H. Ray, "The Rise of the Cultural Creatives," *New Age Journal* (January/February 1997): 74-77, at 75 and Paul H. Ray and Sherry Ruth Anderson, *Culture*

Creatives: How 50 Million People Are Changing the World (New York: Harmony, 2000), 170-204.

6. Michele Galen and Karen West, "Companies Hit the Road Less Traveled," *Business Week* 3427 (June 5, 1995): 82-84, at 83. See also Tom Peters, "Business Leaders Should Be Spirited, Not Spiritual," *Chicago Tribune*, April 5, 1993, Business Section, 8.
7. John P. Kotter, *Leading Change* (Boston: Harvard Business School, 1996), 35-158.
8. Max DePree, *Leadership Jazz* (New York: Dell, 1992), 26.
9. I have drawn on Kendrick B. Melrose, *Making the Grass Greener on Your Side: A CEO's Journey to Leading By Serving* (San Francisco, CA: Berrett-Koehler, 1995); Larry Julian, *God Is My CEO: Following God's Principles in a Bottom-Line World* (Avon, MA: Adams Media, 2001), 192-199; Ken Melrose, "Putting Servant-Leadership into Practice," in *Insights on Leadership: Service, Stewardship, Spirit, and Servant-Leadership*, ed. Larry C. Spears (New York: John Wiley, 1998).
10. Ibid., 279; Melrose, *Grass Greener*, xix.
11. Ibid., 123.
12. Julian, *God*, 194.
13. Melrose, *Grass Greener*, 145.
14. Melrose, "Putting," 285.
15. Ibid (italics omitted).
16. Ibid., 285-286 (italics omitted).
17. Ibid., 286 (italics omitted).
18. Ibid., 287; Melrose, *Grass Greener*, 38-39.
19. Ken Blanchard and Phil Hodges, *The Servant Leader: Transforming Your Heart, Head, Hands & Habits* (Nashville, TN: Countryman, 2003), 66-67.
20. Gregory N.P. Konz and Francis X. Ryan, "Maintaining an Organizational Spirituality: No Easy Task," *Journal of Organizational Management* 12:3 (July 1999): 200-210, at 203-204; Davis, *Managing*, 39-57.
21. I have drawn on Melrose, *Grass Greener*, 43-44, 74, 116-118, 134, 141; Melrose, "Putting," 288-290; Julian, *God*, 196-198.
22. Ibid., 196.
23. Ibid., 198.
24. Melrose, *Grass Greener*, 146; Melrose, "Putting," 293.
25. Melrose, *Grass Greener*, 79-80, 119; Melrose, "Putting," 294; Julian, *God*, 198-199; The Toro Company, U.S. Securities and Exchange Commission, Form 10-K, For Fiscal Year Ended October 31, 2002, 12, 14; The Toro Company, Proxy Statement, January 31, 2003, 15.
26. See, e.g., David Leonhardt, "As Companies Reduce Costs, Pay Is Falling Top to Bottom," *New York Times*, April 26, 2003, B1.
27. Jeffrey Pfeffer, *The Human Equation: Building Profits By Putting People First* (Boston: Harvard Business School, 1998), 5.
28. Julian, *God*, 197. See also Melrose, *Grass Greener*, 161-162.

Selected Bibliography

Books

Darden, Robert and P.J. Richardson, *Corporate Giants: Personal Stories of Faith and Finance* (Grand Rapids, MI: Fleming H. Revell, 2002).

DePree, Max, *Leadership Is an Art* (New York: Dell, 1989).

Greenleaf, Robert K., *Servant Leadership: A Journey into the Nature of Legitimate Power and Greatness* (Mahwah, NJ: Paulist Press, 1977).

Julian, Larry, *God Is My CEO: Following God's Principles in a Bottom-Line World* (Avon, MA: Adams Media, 2002).

Mitroff, Ian I. and Elizabeth A. Denton, *A Spiritual Audit of Corporate America: A Hard Look at Spirituality, Values, and Religion in the Workplace* (San Francisco, CA: Jossey-Bass, 1999).

Nash, Laura L., *Believers in Business* (Nashville, TN: Thomas Nelson, 1994).

Pfeffer, Jeffrey, *The Human Equation: Building Profits By Putting People First* (Boston: Harvard Business School, 1998).

Pollard, C. William, *The Soul of the Firm* (Grand Rapids, MI: Harper Business and Zondervan, 1996).

Articles

Barboza, David, "In This Company's Struggle, God Has Many Proxies," *New York Times*, November 21, 2001, C1.

Gunther, Marc, "God and Business," *Fortune* 144:1 (July 9, 2001): 58-80.

Machalaba, Daniel, "More Employees Are Seeking to Worship God on the Job," *Wall Street Journal*, June 25, 2002, B1.

McGraw, Dan, "The Christian Capitalists," *U.S. News and World Report* 118:10 (March 13, 1995): 52-62.

Index

173